Stepping Stones to Freedom

Dr. Mickey Park, Dminn.

For information contact :
Set Free To Serve Ministries
P.O. Box 253
New Hope, TN 37380
http://www.setfreetoserveministry.org
email: setfree@setfreetoserveministry.org

ISBN: **978-0692873496 (Stepping Stones To Freedom)**

Clippings from the Prison Fellowship Inside Journal
Republished by permission from Prison Fellowship

Book and Cover design by Designer Bethany Park

FORWARD by Stacy Park

Facing possible death row and charged with first degree murder and robbery Mickey's life was seemingly over. Drugs and alcohol had taken its toll on him and right down the deepest darkest path imaginable. He always told himself, "That will never happen to me. I won't ever go to prison" Yet there he was, one wretched and wreaked life facing death row or at best the rest of his natural life in prison.

A person doesn't just wake up one day and get themselves in a situation like this. For Mickey, it was growing up in an environment that seeded and planted a poor mindset. He grew up where alcohol consumption was the norm. Everyone of his uncles drank, his cousins drank and worse than that his own mother was a terrible alcoholic. When he was 3 years old, his biological father went to Tennessee State Penitentiary (Brushy Mountain) and needless to say he grew up without a father which every child so desperately needs. It was a wayward kind of living that started as a young person. A lifestyle, a pattern of making bad choices.

As an elementary and middle school age child he was a rebel and caused trouble wherever he went. Known by the law starting at age 10 for vandalism and stealing. Skipping school and being sent home for fighting was a regular occurrence. At 11 years old he was adjudicated as a juvenile delinquent. Drinking started regular at age 12 and at age 14 he was even arrested for disorderly conduct, which was due to being high on LSD.

By the time Mickey was 15 his life was a real mess and the devil was on his heels. Deeper and deeper into the addiction of drugs and alcohol. At age 17 he literally was kicked out of high school. The principal told him "you don't want to be here, and I sure don't want you to be here so why don't you just leave."

At 18 Mickey joined the United States Army, lying when they asked if he had ever been in trouble. "No sir, never been in trouble" they signed him up and after boot camp he was shipped off to Germany. A free trip to the best place on planet earth for a person that loved drugs and alcohol. While in Germany it was party hardy, let's get high every chance there was. Down, down, down spiraling in a downward fashion.

After the military it was hitch hiking all across the country and into Canada, day in and day out just rallying for a good time. Then Mickey decided to head to Miami in an effort to find his dad who was living a homeless alcoholic on the streets of Miami. Sure enough as the devil would have it, in a city as large as Miami, he was able to find his dad. They spent a number of weeks together on a daily mission to stay high and drunk. After having a big knock down drag out fight Mickey left and headed back to Tennessee.

On his way back to Tennessee he stopped in Destin Florida where the demise of his life would occur. Meeting up with another drugie they were desperate for more drugs and alcohol. Their craving and addiction lead to a robbery that ended in the unthinkable- a terrible murder. This is where living for the devil got them, a highway to hell.

After being arrested and extradited back to Okaloosa County Florida, he was charged with first degree murder and robbery, facing death row or at best the rest of his natural life in prison. His life was over, the buck wild living had come to a screeching halt. It wasn't mama's fault, it wasn't daddy's fault, but it simply was Mickey's fault. There was no one else to blame, he had made the bad choices.

The shame, bitterness, hate and unforgiveness was overtaking him to the point that he decided rather than rot on death row, he would end his own life. On the brink of suicide, he decided to pray one last prayer in memory of his grandmother who was the only Christian influence he had ever had in his life.

It was there on that old dingy solitary confinement jail cell that Mickey prayed a prayer that changed his life. "Dear God, if you are real and I do believe you are Lord, please save me or just let me die." It was then that the tears began to flow from the inner depths of his heart. The jailer didn't come the next day and say, "Come on Mickey you have accepted Jesus, we are letting you out."

No! There are consequences to sin and sometimes those consequences are harsh and hard to face. This was the case with Mickey, after a year in the county jail he was sentenced to 99 years with the sentencing judge retaining 1/3 jurisdiction. Meaning for 33 years the judge would have the final say so on any parole consideration.

Mickey had grown very close to the Lord in that year, he spent every waking hour learning about his new life in Christ and was now having to face the reality of life in prison. His first destination after the reception center was U.C.I. "The Rock" one of the most infamous prisons in the state of Florida. Hard core and known for it's intense evilness. Much to his surprise even in this dark place he found Christian brothers and fellowship that was a sweet experience. He found that there was light and freedom even in one of the darkest places imaginable.

During this time he was writing and ministering to a lot of teens. One girl in particular was living for the Lord and was a young missionary sold out for Christ. For two years they wrote nearly every day and talked on the phone, developing a very close relationship. That young girl happens to be me. In December of 1985 at age 20 while I was in Nigeria West Africa God spoke to me in a mighty way and called me to stand beside Mickey, to be a helpmate and encouragement to him. I returned to the states, and in February of 1986 I moved to Florida to stand beside Mickey and have been by his side ever since. I have seen Mickey face trials, disappointments and struggles, I have seen him overcome, carry on and find victory in the battles of life. I have seen him succeed in life. Whether it be living life in prison nearly 17 years or living on the outside facing the challenges each one of us face. I have seen him work very hard studying for years to eventually graduate with a Doctorate degree in Ministry while in Prison and then when he was out he graduated with a Bachelor's degree in Computer Science.

During our time together, I have always been a priority in Mickey's life. The prison had an industry inside the prison where inmates could work and make a few cents an hour. Mickey would save his money regularly and would send it to me to help pay the phone bill. One time after we first met, he sent me money as a sponsor for one of my mission trips. That was almost unheard of for an inmate to send money to their family. Usually the family was sending them money. He never was and never has been a taker but finds joy in giving and being a provider.

Eventually as time went on and it was more than evident that Mickey was a changed individual the Judge dropped the jurisdiction and the Parole commission finally after nearly 17 years paroled him. Mickey had learned a trade in prison called Computer Aided Drafting (CAD) and Geographic Information Systems (GIS). While at work release, a local engineering firm near where we were living, graciously offered him a position.

From there it only got better, we were blessed with a beautiful daughter and eventually we were able to move back to Tennessee. The mountains that Mickey thought many times he would never see again are now the view we look at every waking day of our lives. We are so blessed.

We both work full time professional jobs, Mickey as a Data Base Administrator and I am a Family Practice Nurse Practitioner. We spend every free moment we have speaking at drug rehabs, prisons, and really any place the Lord opens the door to share what a redeemed life looks like. I have known Mickey for 33 years and have walked beside him for 31 years, I can attest that Mickey is a very simple, humble, honest and very hard working man.

He has dedicated his life to seeing people set free from the bondages of drugs and alcohol and he knows firsthand that there is deliverance through faith in Christ.

God is not a respecter of persons and what he has done for Mickey Park he can and will do for you. It is up to you to allow him to come into your life and make a difference. As you read this book it is my prayer that you will see the life changing power of God through Christ Jesus and that you will learn that what Jeremiah 29:11 says can become a truth for you:

> *"For I know the plans I have for you, says the Lord. They are plans for good and not for evil, to give you a future and a hope." Living Bible.*

Acknowledgements:

This book is truly a team effort of many years and many people that have impacted my life. My wife Stacy and the way she has been a blessing and used of the Lord to stand by my side in the hardest and most difficult times of my life.

The Chaplains and Prison Ministry Volunteers who became not only dear friends but family to Stacy and I. Family like Debbie and Gary Gibbens who loved us and encouraged us in Christ as if we were family. Then the Christian brothers who were there in the fire with us like Rob, Kenny, Cedric, Ernie, John, Don and hundreds of others.

The Prison Ministry preachers like Scott Heburn, Randy and Elizabeth Davenport, Bill Corum, Kenny Cofield that are still in the fight of faith to reach into the prisons and see souls saved and lives changed.

Most of all this book is not about me or what I did, but about Jesus Christ and His glorious miraculous Grace and what He did.

The following Quote from inside my bible from 1986 is still as real today as it was yesterday:

2 Cor. 3:5 "Not that we are sufficient of ourselves to think anything as of ourselves, but our sufficiency is of God" Is my motto for the rest of my life. With every ounce of my being I vow to serve God. By it, in it and through it all. (Dec. 22, 1986 U.C.I "The Rock").

CHAPTERS:

Chapter 1: In the Afterglow of His Glory:

It was an amazing week of Prison Ministry in November as I went into Florida Prisons with a Prison Ministry Team with Scott and Cindy Heburn, Randy and Elizabeth Davenport. I had driven over 950 miles from the Hills of Tennessee to the Panhandle of North Florida to go in over 10 Prisons and share the Hope of the Gospel of Jesus Christ to the men incarcerated behind the Prison Gates and Razor wire. What an awesome time we had. As soon as I got back to Tennessee my Facebook post was:

> ***But thanks be to God, which giveth us the victory through our Lord Jesus Christ. Therefore, my beloved brethren, be ye stedfast, unmoveable, always abounding in the work of the Lord, forasmuch as ye know that your labor is not in vain in the Lord. 1Cor. 15:56-57 THANKS BE TO GOD! We had an amazing weekend of Prison Ministry going to 10 prisons over six days with Scott Heburn Prison Ministry. The Lord moved in a mighty way on the Hearts and Lives of many men as our team shared music and ministry to some 800 prisoners. Please pray for these men whose Lives were touched and forever changed and challenged.***

Team JESUS was sharing Hope and Shining Light in the Darkness.

Now, looking back, it was sort of eerie to be standing outside the fence at the Gate of the Prisons waiting to get checked in and cleared by the security staff. I looked at the Razor Wire and I looked at the Gates, then suddenly memories flashed back in my mind of all the times I had lived on the other side of that razor wire and on the inside of those gates.

I looked at the visiting park and thought of all the visits I had gotten from the love of my life, Stacy my fiancé. How she would stand in line every weekend and go through those gates to visit me. How that visit filled me with the fullness of joy and hope and then how hard it was to see her walk out and have to leave me there in the midst of the razor wire and the high fences.

After one of the services that we had been to and back at the river house where we were staying, I was sitting out on the front porch and that memory of High Fence and Razor Wire flowed through my head. I just began to cry tears. I began to just weep tears from the memories of all the pain and all the hurt that those years behind those fences had brought to me. I could see the men walking the compound and the family visitors sitting there in the visiting park and I felt their pain, I felt their hurt.

Oh! How deeply I felt the hurt of the men who never get visits. I felt the pain of the men that came into the Chapel services. What a burden it was on myself and the rag tag ministry team of ex- convicts and ex-drug addicts I was with. It was our desire to bring Hope and the

Light of Christ to their darkness. I sat there on the front porch in that rocking chair crying and hurting for those prisoners, and I knew that those tears and that hurt in my heart were from the heart of the Lord Jesus Christ who had come into my darkness and my hurting heart in a County Jail years before.

The Glory of the Lord still shines in the darkness of our lives and into the hurting hearts of our souls as we walk with Him in or out of Prison. That was the truth of the ministry and the music that I had encountered as I went back in behind the gates and razor wire. I was in the afterglow of His Love, Mercy and Grace. From that, I realized that He ministers to us ministry volunteers and soldiers of the cross just as much as He ministers to the prisoners that we are going in to share His Hope with. He gives us renewed hope and a renewed fullness and freshness of the Spirit of God. In the afterglow of His Glory we are renewed and refreshed with his Hope and Mercy just like Lamentations 3:22-22 says, "It is of the Lord's mercies that we are not consumed, because his compassions fail not. They are new every morning: great is thy faithfulness. The Lord is my portion, saith my soul; therefore will I hope in him." Yes! Glory to God, they are new every morning.

The Lord's Mercies! They are new every morning. Yes. Praise GOD!

It is through His Mercy and Grace that we breathe the breath we breathe. Like so, so many I have had many close calls and close encounters with death while high and stoned on alcohol and drugs out of my mind. From bar room fights, fighting over drugs or dope money, or from car wrecks while D.U.I. with all the cars totaled out. On the very door step of Hell. Yet, God had his hand of Grace on me. I can look back and see in that rear view mirror of my life that God had his angels watching out for me. They were there even when I was running with the devil and running as hard as I could from His Love, Mercy and Grace. Jesus Christ was reaching out for me.

"JESUS TEAM": Scott&Cindy Heburn, Ernie Seltzer, Mickey Randy&Elizebeth Davenport.

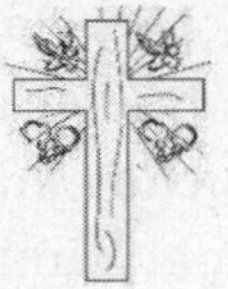

Chapter 2: A Broken Home, Broken Childhood, Broken Life

I come from a broken home, in the inner city of Chattanooga, Tennessee. My dad went to Tennessee State Penitentiary (Brushy Mountain) when I was three years old, mother divorced him and remarried her 2nd husband for the 2nd time. My mother was a chronic alcoholic. My home life was horrific. I recall nothing but bad memories of holidays and her drunken episodes destroying whatever little bit of Christmas my half-sister, my half-brother and I had.

Like many at-risk-youth, all three of us came from different dads. I was the youngest, my sister Linda the oldest and my brother Mike four years older than me. Mother was drinking most of the time, and our only reprieve in our young lives was when we were able to live with our Grandmother and Grandfather. My mom's mother and dad. They were our only sanctuary from the hell of alcoholic fights and drunken rampages.

Even when we were at our grandparents, the uncles or mother would still show up drunk, and there were always drunken fights and arguments. For us, this was every weekend, and it became a normal and expected part of my life.

In the third grade, I remember one time my cousin Danette and I seeing my mother passed out on the couch with whiskey bottles and beer cans all around. We went and took all the whiskey and cans of beer and poured it down the kitchen sink. Thinking in my 3rd grade elementary school mind that by doing so it would solve the problem and help stop mamma from being drunk. Sadly that did not work. She only got up and went and got more liquor and beer and started all over again. It was more than just whiskey and beer that went down the drain; it was my childhood, my hopes, my dreams, my life.

It was around this time that my stepdad decided to move to Pittsburgh, Pennsylvania to work on a big construction job. He was an IBEW Union Electrician, and in 1967-68 there were a lot of steel mills being built and large construction projects going on there. At this same time, my sister Linda had found her way to escape the crazy mess of our home life. She got pregnant at 16. My mother and stepdad kicked her out, and she ended up living with our grandparents. Then by his luck of the draw, somehow my brother Mike was able to convince our Aunt Susie and Uncle Dan to take him in and let him stay in Chattanooga to go to school. Good for them, but bad for me. I would be the only one they took with them. I dreaded the thought of that and hated to leave my family and friends in Tennessee.

In Pittsburg, I would start the 4th grade at Mckees Rock Elementary School. I hated every day of it. The kids would make fun of me because of my southern hillbilly accent. I would have to fight almost every day some big bully kid in the 5th or 6th grade who thought it was a fun past time to make fun of me. I would fight and scrap with all I had and beat those kids off of me. I would hit them with a brick or a stick or whatever I could get my hands on. Their parents would go to my stepdad and complain, and he would cuss them out and tell them the little punks got what they deserved.

I hated my life; I hated living in this awful place in Pittsburg without my family in Tennessee. I had no friends, no family and had to literally fight every day to survive. After school, I would come home to a dingy apartment with an alcoholic mother passed out on the couch. My step dad would be at work building the steel mill. He worked long hours and pulled double shifts trying to make money and probably stay away from mom. Who could blame him? He was not mean to me, and really he was as trapped as I was. He had married a woman he loved, but who loved alcohol more than she loved herself, anything or anyone.

There was a lot of days I would come home from school and mother would be passed out on the couch. She would have nothing cooked to eat. I become an expert at Peanut Butter and Jelly sandwiches. I could make them with bananas, jelly, two layers or three layers. On some days that would become my breakfast, school lunch and dinner.

At school, I did so poorly in class that I believe my teachers actually knew something was horribly wrong at home. I didn't pay much attention in class or really care too much about what they were teaching. I had to worry about fighting my way home after school and wondering how my mother would be once I got home. Who cared about the Revolutionary War or Independence? I had my own war and battles to fight.

At the apartment, there was this one bully kid

that lived downstairs, and he would pick on me and make fun of my southern hillbilly accent. I would mock his Yankee accent and let him know he didn't talk so proper as well. He cornered me one day in the hallway by the stairs, and I had just about had enough of him and his bullying me so I punched him in the face with all I had and pushed him as hard as I could off of me. Down the stairs, he rolled like a fat little Pillsbury dough boy. When his folks got a hold of my stepdad, he told them to keep their 6th-grade kid away from me, and I wouldn't hurt him.

Then one day mother told me to stay home from school and to pack up all my clothes. She was drunk as cooter brown and giddy, so I knew she was up to something.

She had me give her my little red teddy bear, and I watched her take some scissors and cut open his back stitching, and she stuffed a big wad of money in him and sewed him back up. She had gone to the bank and withdrew all of the funds and was stashing the cash in the teddy. She called a cab and her and I went to the train station and got on a train to Chattanooga. My poor old stepdad didn't have a clue about any of it. All he had when we came home that night was an empty house, some bread, peanut butter and jelly.

Once back home in Chattanooga and back at my grandparents I was the happiest hillbilly kid in the Hills of Tennessee. It felt so good to be back home. My old friends, my cousins, uncles, aunts, brother and sister. I had been through hell in life up there all alone having to fight and scrap and survive. I was so happy to be home.

I was in the 4th Grade and even then I would start

a fight and get into trouble at school. It was hard to be normal when you grew up in an abnormal home life. It was hard to be a kid when you had to face so many hard and harsh things that most adults never face. Having to come home to a alcoholic mother, or having no father figure. There was no "man of the house" in my house. It was just me, my drunk mother and a bottle of whiskey.

Mother rented us a small house down the street from my Grandparents and got me enrolled in 4th Grade. One day coming home from Clifton Hills Elementary School, I remember walking into the front door and seeing my mom there laid up on the couch half naked with some strange man. They were both disgustingly drunk. Whiskey bottles, beer cans and cigarette butts all over the place. I ran out on the porch and grabbed a big stick and came in swinging. I was gonna crack that old drunk dude like a walnut. He ran out the door and jumped in his car and left. But the pain was still there. The damage was done. I was so hurt, so angry and mad. I was so hurt and so full of the pain and so sick of this messed up life I kept coming home too. A Broken Home, A Broken Childhood, A Broken Life.

Chapter 3: A Juvenile Delinquent

Eventually, my mom and stepdad made up and got back together. He came back to Chattanooga, and they started over. By this time I had been running with the neighborhood boys, and we were terrorizing the entire neighborhood. Fighting in school and after school trying to prove we were the toughest kids of the neighborhood. Me and my two best buddies who were brothers ran around like little outlaws in a wild wild west movie.

We would go to the local grocery store and knock stuff off the shelves or steal candy bars and drinks and make the bag boys chase us up the street as we would laugh and out run them down along the railroad tracks. There used to be an old saying that you grew up on the wrong side of the tracks. That was certainly true of us. We were poor and grew up in the roughest neighborhoods of drugs and alcohol infested areas of the inner city of Chattanooga, Tennessee.

We were in trouble all the time for mischief and just pure meanness. We would knock out the street lights, or tie ropes to the bumpers of cars then to the garbage cans and watch the neighbor guy drive off to work dragging the garbage can down the street. All the while hiding in the bushes watching and laughing our fool heads off. We would throw rocks at cars, or go to the laundromat and shoot out all the light bulbs with our bb guns. We would go outside in the back of the grocery store and pull over all the metal milk crates that they stacked up and watch them fall like giant pine trees onto cars and trucks.

The Grocery store and some neighbors finally filed charges with the Juvenile Court, and they ended up adjudicating us juvenile delinquents as 4th graders. Shortly after this my mom and step dad took me and moved across the State Line to Georgia so the charges would never amount to anything. Mother kept drinking, and I kept running with the rowdy boys that I could find.

My step dad worked all the time and mother worked some. I ended up going to my grandmothers more and more to be close to my best buddies. We would hang out with my Uncle Johnny, who was a chronic alcoholic. He would drive around the neighborhood until 3 or 4 am in the morning drinking beer. He worked at an Auto Body Shop repair place, and he drank all the time. He would give me a cold bottle of beer and let me drink one. I was only in the 5th grade of elementary school. By the time I was in the 6th and 7th grade my buddies and I were drinking, smoking pot and running with the big dogs. We were all big for our age and anxious to prove it. We were sitting on bar stools drinking with our uncles and older cousins. We were drinking, smoking pot and fighting in the bars and parking lots every Friday and Saturday night. It was sort of a family tradition. Kind of like that old Hank Williams song. "Hank why do you roll that smoke, why do you drink that drink, well it's just a family tradition."

In a similar sense so was prison, jails, and trouble with the law. My buddies' oldest brother was in Prison while we were growing up. Although my dad had gotten out of prison when I was 5 years old, he would only come around every few months or so. Several of my cousins ended up in county jail and having to go to the Silverdale Work House for a while.

I recall one time in the 1st grade when my dad came by Grandma's and got me and took me for a day. We went all over town and he had me go in the grocery stores and buy up 5 and 10 pound bags of sugar. I had no clue what he was doing. When he took me back to Grandma and left, she asked what all we did today and I told her "we bought bags and bags of sugar". She shouted Oh! My Lord! They're making moonshine somewhere! Sure enough my dad and Uncle Junior were cooking up a batch of moonshine up on the mountain.

As I got older when he was around, my dad would give us pot or buy us beer. He took us to pool halls and would let us do whatever we wanted. He was just another alcoholic and was helping us keep on that family tradition. He was just helping me ride on that Highway to Hell.

The stepping stones to prison often begins as a small stepping stone and takes just one step at a time to get there. My steps to prison begins early and even as a 9 or 10-year-old juvenile I was in and out of trouble. It was a way of acting out, and even crying out in a sense for help. But no one could help me. We were what the smart folks and the Juvenile Judges called incorrigible. *Beyond correcting, improving, or changing*.

Vandalism and malicious mischief are what the Juvenile Court called it as they adjudicated me a juvenile delinquent. As we grew older we all started drinking alcohol and doing drugs. All of our parents, uncles, and cousins drank, so it was just the next step for me to start drinking beer at 12 and 13 years old. We would steal beer from our parents, or our drunk uncles. Once we got a little older we would mow lawns to get money for beer. By the time I was 13 and 14 I was smoking pot and experimenting with drugs. It was easy to get pot, it was easy to get pills in the inner city. I remember at 14 years old being transported to the county jail while high on an LSD trip. My life was totally out of control even before it had really started.

In Psychology there is a concept called self-fulfilling prophecy. This is where something is told to you over and over until it actually becomes true. My step dad used to berate me and tell me that I would end up just like my dad one day. Which for me, it meant I would end up a drug addict alcoholic and in prison just like my dad. How true that prophetic word would become.

After the LSD high at 14 years old my stepdad kicked me out and I had to go live with my sister Linda and her husband in Walker County in Rock Springs, Georgia. I finished 8th grade and stayed with my sister. She let me drink and she was a hard core alcoholic just like our mom. By then I had turned 15 and that summer I left her place and went to my grandmother's. I was hanging out with some bad dudes and even did a strong armed robbery with one of them. Then my dad came in town from Miami, Florida and I decided I would go back to Miami with him.

At 15 years old I hitchhiked from Chattanooga, Tennessee to Miami, Florida with my ex-con, hippie, dope addict, alcoholic dad Mack Mickle Park. I learned that you could stay high for days on the road. People would pick you up and give you booze and dope and how life was just a big party.

Miami was a humongous city and larger than anything I had ever seen. I had never heard of a Cuban or ever seen a Hispanic person. I was a hillbilly country bumpkin kid in the big city. It was full of tall buildings, coconut trees, and city lights. We spent a lot of time on Miami Beach and in that party crowd.

My dad had a few friends we stayed with, and he worked a few odd jobs to get us some money to live and drink on. We all just stayed high. That was more important than food or rent or anything. After a few months, I decided I wanted to get back home to Tennessee, I was homesick. I was not up to this Miami life, so my dad had bought a little old car and we drove back to Chattanooga.

Once back to Tennessee I stayed with my grandmother, and shortly later my dad went back to Miami. I started the 9th grade at East Lake Junior High and continued to live the life of a Juvenile Delinquent, in and out of trouble, fighting, smoking pot and drinking. I would walk the halls and look for some boy just to bust up and scrap with. I wanted to make a reputation for myself and I would start fights on the steps of the school just for fun. I believe I made straight "F's" that year and yet they passed me on to the 10th grade. I didn't care about grades, all I cared about was drinking, partying, girls, good dope and a lot of booze.

I entered into the 10th Grade at Kirkman Technical High School which was an inner-city vocational technical school located in downtown Chattanooga. With that rowdy attitude and full blown drug and alcohol dependency, it was not a good fit. I skipped almost all the classes, made straight "F's" and hit the local downtown bars and pool halls. The day after a fight with one of the star football player boys, whom I had beat like a volleyball from one end of the bus to the other, the Assistant Principal called me into his office and told me, son, you don't want to be here, and I sure don't want you here, so you just need to leave. I didn't drop out of High School, I was kicked out. A Juvenile Delinquent with a Capital D. My life was a total failure, pop another pill and take another toke.

Drugs and alcohol addiction will destroy dreams, destinies and futures. It will rob one of a life and leave one empty on a road to nowhere. It often can start out as a youthful game of life, but will deceitfully take full control of one's young life and bring nothing but failure and destruction.

Mickey 10 year old "At-Risk-Youth"

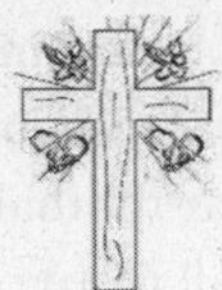

Chapter 4: Miami and Tequila Time

My life was sort of just drifting so where does a 17-year-old dope addict alcoholic go after getting kicked out of High School. Why not go hang out with his ex-con dad down in Miami so he can party and keep the good times rolling. So I caught a Greyhound Bus to Miami and got up with my dad. He had a place with some people who would let us stay there. They were all alcoholics, and everyone just worked enough to keep the booze flowing, and the rent paid. I didn't intend to look for a job; I just wanted to party and hang out and enjoy the ride.

I would turn 18 in Miami, and it was all just a big party. We were all into drinking high dollar scotch that we would steal from the neighbor who got a V.A. Check every month, we also were drinking Tequila and smoking weed.

Several of the girls in the apartment complex were hard core junkies. This was where I first saw someone actually shoot up dope. They would shoot up heroin and coke or whatever they could get a hold of. I was horrified and sickened at watching them shoot drugs and how heroin would just wipe them totally out, I kept telling myself Oh! No! That will never happen to me. No way will I ever go that low or that far as to stick a needle in my arm. "No way!"

It was this time in Miami that I first saw a girl

shoot drugs into the vein of her neck because she had used up all the veins in her arms. They lived in the apartment behind us, and I would hang out over there smoking pot and drinking with all of them and watch them shoot dope. I was not into that myself and was just fine with sipping my tequila and smoking my weed. I didn't want to get into the heroin or the cocaine but give me a few pills like Quaaludes or Dilaudids or some Valiums and I was all in.

It was a big city and I learned how to survive in the jungle with these dope addicts. We would go over to the housing projects and they would buy their dope from the dope man. Then they would go back and shoot up. Their boyfriends would steal and rob whatever they could to keep the dope money flowing. I was just a bystander on the beachside of life watching them destroy their lives with hard core dope. Several times the ambulance and paramedics would come and haul one of them to the hospital with an overdose. They would get out a few days later and be right back at the ratty apartment shooting up more dope. I was just living my life smoking pot drinking tequila and staying high and drunk. An empty and desolate life.

One night me and one of the dudes from the apartment were hanging out on the corner and this guy comes up and he had some pot, so we are smoking his dope and drinking our beer. The guy was young maybe 19 or so and seemed to maybe have a little money. So me and my buddy decide let's rob him, so we take him for a ride out by the Miami Beach causeway, and pull over and beat the dude up and throw him in the Biscayne Bay. We take the money and go get some pot and more beer and go to the apartment and party on.

Around about 4:00 am the time when the neighbors Cuban rooster would crow the Miami Cops are kicking on the door of the apartment and someone opens it and they rush in and drag my buddy and me out and off to the Dade County Jail. The dude that we had robbed had told them where we were and they busted both of us for Aggravated Assault and Strong Armed Robbery.

I woke up the next morning hungover and in total shock. This was not the Chattanooga City jail or any of those little country bumpkin jails I had been in and out of back home. This was a God awful place and here I was 18 years old and just a dumb old hillbilly from Tennessee. Needless to say, my buddy was only 17, and he was in juvie, but now I was no longer a Juvenile and somehow I had missed that memo.

Miami-Dade County Jail was BIG! I mean it was enormous and it was full. I was scared to death. What a mess I had gotten myself into now. They booked me in and told me that I am charged with Aggravated Assault and Strong Armed Robbery and that in Florida that can carry up from 5 to 25 years. All of this had to be a big mistake, a bad dream, a bad high. I did not intend to end up in Miami-Dade County Jail facing serious prison time. I had just barely turned 18. It was only a few weeks into my 18th year, and 1975 was supposed to be a great year.

The situation was critical and my old man was out there with no bond money, and no lawyer and no way to help me. What a mess I had gotten myself into, how was I going to get out of this nightmare? I had never spent more than a night in jail, and it was like a sleepover before, sort of like the Andy Griffith shows and Otis. I always sobered up and they let me out. Well, not this time. It was Miami and it was not looking good for me. I needed help and boy I needed HELP in a BIG WAY.

I was laying in my bunk in a cell with several young black dudes and a few white boys. They were all youthful offenders and had a lot of street smarts. One of the black kids was talking with me, and I told him my case and he told me that man God can help you if you let him. He gave me a Bible and I crawled up in my top bunk and started to read some of it. I read in Matthew about Jesus and the miracles he was doing. I didn't know much about Jesus, or the Bible but I needed His help, and this was the only help I had at the moment. I would read that Bible and pray and beg God; please get me out this mess. If I can get out of this I will live for you Lord; I will be whatever you want. I am sorry, Oh! God, I am so sorry!

Yep, I was for sure sorry alright, sorry I got caught. But I sure needed some Devine help now if I had ever needed any. That must be what they call Jailhouse Religion because here I was in the jail house and I sure was wanting to tap into that Religion if it would help me. I needed God's help, and I needed it now.

As crazy as it seemed I read and prayed and asked God and pleaded with God to please help me. Oh! Dear Lord, I am 18 years old, I am still a baby, don't let them send me to Prison with all those baby rapers and killers. Please help me, God. I laid up there in that jail bunk in the Miami-Dade County jail and read that Bible and prayed everyday for like three days waiting on the Preliminary hearing.

The time of the hearing day came closer, and I read the passage about how when they would bring you before Magistrates and Judges that for you to take no thought for what you shall say, but that the Holy Spirit would speak for you. That was crazy to me, but hey it was in the Bible, and that must mean something. This old Hillbilly was out of aces, and all I had was a hand full of deuces, so I would gamble on God helping me before anything else.

The morning before the hearing I was laying there in the bed waiting for Court Call and I heard a voice. I heard this soft still voice speak to me, and say "Mickey by 11:00 o'clock you will be out of here today!" I starting shaking and shivering with goosebumps and fear. What was that? I thought. Shortly after they called for Court Call and I was taken out from the cell for the court call.

Once in the courtroom, I saw they had the boy sitting there that we had beat up and robbed. From what I could tell he didn't look too banged up. I mean it could've been worse. There was my dad and some of the folks from the apartment even my juvie buddy was sitting in the audience with them. He was already out on bond.

They call my name, and I step up to the table and sit down. The Judge asks me if I wish to have a public defender represent me and that this is an evidentiary preliminary hearing. I tell the Judge "No Sir" I do not want a lawyer at this time. Then I ask the judge if I can ask the victim some questions? He says yes you may, and I honestly do not know where or how but I began to ask the guy some questions. Did I at any time hit you? Or did I at any time have a weapon? And did I not try to keep the other boy from hurting you? And the guy answered and said no he did not recall me hitting him, but the other boy did, and that no I did not have a weapon, and that I did try to stop the boy at one time. Well, then the Judge takes his little wooden hammer and hits the desk and says ***"it appears that we have the wrong man, case dismissed!"***

The lawyers in the courtroom were all coming up to me afterward shaking my hand, and telling me I should go to law school and become a lawyer. It was amazing. I was processed out and as I walked out of the Court House I looked up at a big old wall clock in the lobby there at the Miami-Dade County Court House and it read 10 minutes till 11:00. I was in total awe and knew deep in my heart and soul that God had worked all this out for me. That it was some sort of miracle but I just couldn't process it. I couldn't comprehend or truly appreciate what had just occurred.

I left that Miami-Dade County Court House and went off with my dad and the bunch of friends and the juvie buddy to get high, drunk and go right back to the same old lifestyle. That is where Jailhouse religion gets you. Nowhere! I walked away from a 2nd chance and the God of second chances. But I would never forget that it was God who helped me in that Miami-Dade County Jail and what happened that day. There is a real God, and beyond the tequila and the drugs, He is there for us.

Mickey as young boy

Mickey 10th Grade

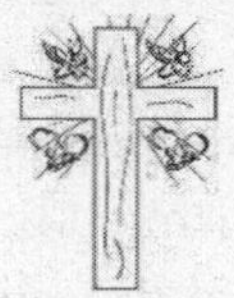

Chapter 5: Home Again

After the ordeal with the robbery and jail, my dad and his friends moved out of the neighborhood to a different place. At least we got away from that crowing rooster. We had thought about killing it and cooking it but never got around to it. Now here we were in a different apartment, same old lifestyle of partying and drinking. I was smoking weed and drinking all the time, really not sure where my life was heading. Sort of lost and confused and just in a fog of drugs and alcohol. I had chilled out some. I did not want a repeat of the Miami-Dade County Jail, but I had no real direction or goals in my life. At 18 years old I had been kicked out of High School, almost went to Florida Prison and was not sure what to do with my life. It was an era of confusion and a lost and directionless life.

I would lay out by the pool at the apartment and think maybe I should go back to Chattanooga. Maybe I should join the military or get a GED and go to college. I wanted to do something more with my life than what I was doing but just didn't know what or how. I was not really into God or had not given much thought to God since I left that courtroom that day, but I did believe He was real and all. I just didn't know Him or really know how to know Him. All I knew was getting high and getting drunk. My gods were drugs, sex and rock-n-roll. My dad was an atheist or agnostic and really was stoned or high all the time. He sure did not have any connection to God.

Life was confusing. I had not had any contact with my mother or grandmother or anyone from Tennessee for several months. I had hoped that I would be able to make it on my own in Miami and just find a life. Well, that wasn't happening.

I was laying out by the pool one day, and some chick leaned over the balcony and said, “Hey are you, Mickey?” I thought wow how did she know my name? I told her, yes, and she said: "your mother just called and wanted you to call her in Tennessee." I was like wow dude that is so weird. How did my mom get her phone number and what was going on?

So I go and call my mom, and she explains that she had been calling the police stations and everywhere looking for me. Somehow she got the info for the apartment complex and was able to find the number of someone who lived there and called them to try and get in touch with me. She shared that her and my stepdad had been going to a little Baptist Church out by their house, and that they had both gotten "Saved" (whatever that meant) and that my stepdad wanted to restore our relationship and wanted me to come home. I was stunned and for sure shocked. This God of 2nd Chances was for real apparently, even if I didn't fully comprehend it.

My mom sent me a bus ticket and I caught a Greyhound bus back home to good old Chattanooga, Tennessee. I moved back in with my mom and stepdad, and I could sense that things were different. They both had a glow and a joy. The house felt peaceful and calm. Mother was not drinking, and the stepdad was not being mean and hateful. They had a joy in their lives I had never seen before. They were going to Mount Vernon Baptist Church in the Keith community of Ringgold, Georgia. They were even involved in a children's Sunday School Bus Ministry. They were happy and I was glad for them but it was all weird and not for me. I felt I had gone too far and was beyond ever being any goody, goody Church boy.

It was good that they had Jesus now, but as for me I was not there yet, I felt it wasn't for me, I was beyond His Grace, beyond His Love. There were times when I did go to church with them and the preacher or evangelist would give an altar call after the message and I would stand there holding the pews so tight my knuckles turned white. I wouldn't go forward. Even though I felt Christ calling me, and tugging at my hurting heart, I said no and I resisted His loving call of Grace. Not long after this I started going back over to my grandmothers and hanging out with my old friends and getting drunk and high.

One night me and a buddy broke into a liquor store and stole several cases of whiskey. We were so drunk we ended up ditching it on someone's front porch. After a few days, I knew that the law would probably have warrants for us. So I told my friend that maybe we should join the Army, to beat going to jail. He wasn't game, but I thought I would at least try. I told my step dad and he had been in the Marine Corps, so he thought it was a good idea for me. So I went to the Army Recruiter and he had me go get a GED and then signed me up for the Army.

When the recruiter asked had I ever been in any legal trouble I lied and told him "Oh! No sir. Not any." So they let me sign the papers and got me processed and I took the Army Oath of enlistment and became G.I. Mickey. A new adventure and a lot of new experiences awaited me.

Mickey 18 Years Old Before leaving
For the U. S. Army

U.S. Army 1975

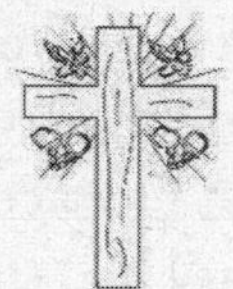

Chapter 6: U.S. Army

The Army loaded me on a bus to Ft. Knox, Kentucky for Basic Training. I was 18 years old and had not worked out a day in my life. The heaviest thing I usually lifted was a cold bottle of beer or a jug of whiskey. I had no idea of what I was going to do or if I would make it through the U.S. Army boot camp. A drill sergeant got all of us in a circle and starting yelling and shouting and I thought "Oh My God, I am like Gomer Pyle in a hot mess." But I had determined that I would give it all I had. I did what they told me, and some of the boys in the unit helped me pull through, and somehow I made it. I think I was surprised that I survived. Surprised that I made it.

After Basic Training I was awaiting orders to go to advanced training when the Captain called me in his office. He said “Park, Hamilton County Tennessee has about a half dozen warrants on you for drunk and disorderly, D.U.I., and theft of property.” I acted shocked and totally surprised. I told him there must be a mistake. I don’t know what is going on.

The Army had me charged with fraudulent enlistment. The Captain then did something very few people had ever done in my life. He went to bat for me. He said “Park your sergeants all say you have worked hard and have really done well. I am going to see what I can do for you." He wrote that I was an exemplary soldier and had proven my commitment to honor the U.S. Army. They let me stay in the service. This was the first time in my life that I had completed anything, the first time in my life that I had succeed in something that I had started.

After basic training I was sent to Ft. Gordon, Georgia for Electronic Communications Equipment Training. Once there I quickly got up with the party crowd and found the guys to run around with that loved to drink and smoke dope. Life was still just a big party-hearty lifestyle. We drank all night, smoked all the dope we could and still made it through the program somehow.

After training at Ft. Gordon the Army did something really crazy, they gave me orders to Germany. Of all places to send a hillbilly alcoholic drug addict, Germany! That place is world famous for its German Beer. It is world famous for its German people who love to party. The party life in Germany was like no other. It was wild and crazy. Germany had better beer, and they had better dope. Over there I got introduced to Hashish fresh from Lebanon, and also brown heroin from the fields of Afghanistan. I was smoking all the hash I could get my hands on and snorting pure heroin while listening to Jimi Hendrix music all night long.

I will never forget how one night our Battalion was out in the field during Army maneuvers and we were posted up on a mountain in Kaiserslautern with our microwave communications truck to support the communications system for the command. A bunch of my GI buddies were all piled in my communications van smoking a big bong of Lebanese hashish and then there is this hard knock on the van door and I open it and smoke billowed out like a Cheech & Chong movie and there was our platoon sergeant getting hit in the face with a big billow of our smoke. He just shut the door and walked off cussing and shaking his head.

It was just a big party. It did not take me long to find some German friends and soldiers that lived for the same high, and that lived for the same Satan and walked in the same Satanic darkness of addiction. Before long I also was running a black market from the PX on the Military bases where I would buy cigarettes and Jim Bean whiskey at the military discount and take it off base and resale to the comrades and German locals at twice and triple the price.

It was easy to take the black market business up a notch and start dealing drugs. I would buy heroin and hash and resell it to the soldiers on the base. I was not a very good dope man or business man as I ended up smoking more dope than I would sell. I smoked all the profits. I had also started sniffing heroin. Myself and a few buddies from around Atlanta, Georgia spent almost the entire three years over there getting high and partying with the Germans. I went to the Swiss Alps, to the Austrian-Bavarian Mountains, to Munich, to the Black Forest, to Heidelberg and all those cool places to party.

Drinking, fighting and partying just as if I was back home in Chattanooga. Wild and crazy and totally out of control. One night totally drunk driving back to the barracks I passed out and hit a big ditch and the car careened into a big field. The car almost flipped over and I was thrown from one side to the other like a tennis ball my head was banging against the door frames of the car. I thought it would never stop; I thought I was going to die and this was it for me. Again those angels of God were watching out for this old drunk hillbilly. I woke up with the car steaming and smoking and crawled out and walked away with hardly a scratch. God was watching out for me even when I didn't realize it.

The Army was good to me. It was something that I actually enjoyed as a job. I could have made a career out of it. I even won soldier of the month several times at Company level and even Battalion level and runner-up for Brigade soldier of the month. But the partying and wild lifestyle was more appealing to me than a career. I just wanted to party and get high who cares about a military career. The foolish choices that one makes, can really cause them to regret those poor decisions for the rest of their life sometimes. God was with me, even in the darkness and loneliness of Germany. I know God spared my life that night on that German highway in that car wreck.

Another amazing thing that happened right before I left Germany was one of those old drinking and dope smoking buddies from Atlanta got involved in a small missionary group and got saved and was living for the Lord. Woody would drink as hard and smoke dope as much as any of us, yet here he was now running around like some sort of Jesus freak. I went to the missionary church with him a few times. At one of those meetings I heard about Christ and even got baptized by that missionary group there in a small lake in Germany. I knew about Christ, but I didn't really know Him. After that, I stopped partying, and it wasn't long after that I completed my tour and was Honorably Discharged and came home from Germany.

Getting out of the Army from Germany, I flew into Chattanooga and stayed at my mother and stepdad's home, and I had a love for Jesus in my heart. I wanted to live for Him. I enrolled in Community College on the GI Bill and hoped to get a job while I started this new life. Mother bought me a new Thompson Chain Reference Study Bible and even had my name engraved on it. I had a desire, but the passion and sincerity was not there yet.

Shortly after coming home from Germany and the Army I once again started to hang out with some old friends and at first just get a few beers, then smoked a little pot. Here I was a divorced broken alcoholic who had lost a family and two daughters in a failed teenage marriage built on that lifestyle of drugs and alcohol. The girls lives were damaged from the very start, collateral damage from two teenage drug addicts, alcoholics who could not take care of themselves much less raise two children. I recall how in Germany we would be smoking bongs of hashish and blow the smoke into the face of our 2 year old daughter and laugh as if it was some sort of game. Due to the fact we were both unfit parents I made sure as part of the divorce the girls were adopted out to my ex-wife's family, her mom and an aunt. They deserved better, but unfortunately didn't get it.

It was not long after getting back home that my ex-wife called and asked if I wanted to come over and see my daughter at her mom's. It was so painful to sit there and realize that as I held my 3 year old daughter that I had lost a family. I had destroyed a family with drugs and alcohol just like my mother and father did to me. From there I walked away from the light of Christ and walked right back into the Satanic darkness of my past. I went and got drunk and stoned and as high on dope as the dope would take me. Trying to kill the pain. But nothing could kill that pain.

That is the reality of addiction, it is a vain attempt to kill the pain. Whatever that pain may be, it may not be just physical pain, but the deep, deep emotional pain and hurts in one's life. It is also trying to kill spiritual pain, and to fill that spiritual void in life that in the end does nothing but causes more emptiness and pain.

Chapter 7: From the Light to the Darkness

Being back in Chattanooga and trying to go to College and trying to stay out of trouble was a real struggle for me. You see living clean and sober just wasn't normal for me. It was not too long before I was running with my old friends and back to drinking and smoking pot as hard as ever. Mother was taking care of grandmother as she was suffering from Alzheimer's. I was drinking and partying and in school just to draw the VA Check. My life was totally out of control. Once again all the time stoned or blitzed and on a directionless life, one high to the next.

One morning I got a call from my mother, and she was crying and asked that I come to the Hospital where grandmother was. I staggered into that Hospital room, still high from all night partying. Mother was standing over the bed and there laid my grandmother, Allie May Boyd. She had been the only Christian influence in this entire family. She was a little Pentecostal lady, and she loved the Lord yet every one of her sons, her daughter and about every one of the grandsons and granddaughters were drunks and drug addicts. We grew up in the inner city, and that was the lifestyle that was the family tradition.

Mother and I stood there and in came grandma's Pentecostal preacher. I guess grandma had asked mother to call him to come before she had become unconscious. He came up to her and laid his hand on her and started praying. He was praying some in tongues, and I was standing at the foot of the bed watching with my drug buzzed hungover head bowed. Then I looked at grandma and noticed she had stopped breathing. He finished his prayer, and I said, "she's not breathing!" Mother ran out and grabbed a nurse, and they rushed us all out. Shortly after they came out and told us in the hallway that she was gone. Grandma went Home on a Prayer, and that moment would always be real and imprinted deep in my heart.

Not long after the funeral for my grandmother, I was with Mother, and she wanted to go to her brother's house to my uncle Johnny's. Johnny Boyd was a World War 2 Veteran, he was an alcoholic and had been drinking hard ever since grandmother's funeral. He also was very sick and had stage 4 cirrhosis of the liver because of alcoholism.

Mother pulled up there, and he came out of the house in the driveway, and he had a cold beer in his hand. She was crying and pleading with Uncle Johnny to please, to please stop drinking and let Jesus help him. I watched as he took a big swig of beer and told her "I don't need your Jesus, now get off my property and leave me the hell alone!"

Mother and I drove off, and less than about two weeks later I would be sitting at Erlanger Hospital in Chattanooga with Uncle Johnny's daughter Susie. She and I watched Uncle Johnny die of hard core alcoholism. He had survived the battles of World War 2 but would not survive the battle of Alcoholism.

I went home and got drunk and never made it to the funeral. Shortly before that funeral, our Uncle Dan passed away after a short battle with cancer. He too was an alcoholic and had drank up to his last breath. Myself and some cousins were asked to be the pallbearers and carry his casket to the gravesite. I remember all three of us getting in my cousin Wayne's car and while following the hearse to the gravesite sharing a bottle of Tennessee whiskey. We were all staggering and stumbling as we carried the coffin with good ol' Uncle Dan to the grave site. Thank God we didn't drop him, but we were all drunk and totally blitzed.

After those funerals and all that pain and loss, I remember trying in vain to kill the pain, I just drank harder and drifted deeper into the darkness of addiction. I got several D.U.I.'s, and was in several hit and run car wrecks while drunk. In and out of every County Jail in the area. My life was totally out of control. I had a cousin drive me up to Murfreesboro, Tennessee to a V.A. Hospital and I checked in to their Alcoholic Detox and Drug Recovery Program. The Alcohol Program that the V.A. had was supposed to be one of the best available in this Nation. They tried to help me with the best V.A. doctors and their Alcoholic program. But, they couldn't fix me. I needed JESUS.

A Vietnam vet and I would sit out on the grounds and call a taxi cab and give that cab driver 20 bucks to go to town and buy us a pint of liquor and bring it back. I got violently drunk and ended up in an alcoholic blackout while in the best V.A. Detox Program in the State. They quickly realized they could not fix me, and they kicked me out.

Then I called that same taxi cab driver and talked him into driving me to Chattanooga. I promised him I had a V.A. Check at my house and that he would get paid. He drove me the 80 miles to Chattanooga, and I had him pull up at my drunk uncle Junior's house. I got out went through the front door and ran out the back door. I never paid that taxi cab drive a dime. By the time he called the police I was long gone.

The V.A. Hospital in Murfreesboro was unable to fix me, and now I had a bunch of warrants for D.U.I.'s and hit and runs so I decided I needed a vacation in Miami to let the heat cool off in Chattanooga. I hitchhiked down to Miami to hang out with my dad.

My dad was living just north of Miami in the town of Tamarac in Broward County outside of Ft. Lauderdale. He worked odd jobs, painting or doing light construction and had a small monthly V.A. check to help support him. My dad Mack Mickle Park was a U.S. Marine Korean War Veteran. He had joined at 17 and ended up in the battle of Chosin Reservoir. This was where about 130,000 Chinese and North Korean soldiers surround about 30,000 U.S. Army soldiers and Marines. They were going to annihilate the US forces. General Douglas MacArthur devised a plan to rescue those men if they could fight their way to the coast and he would have Navy amphibious ships there to rescue them. They fought their way out of Chosin Reservoir and made it to the safety of the Navy Amphibious ships. My dad survived the battle of Chosin Reservoir, but he would never survive the battle of drugs and alcohol addiction.

Once back in Florida it was the same old same old routine of partying, drinking and drugging. One night while high at the apartment, another kid and I got into an argument over a dime bag of weed. We started fighting and knocking stuff over. Then he ran into the kitchen and grabbed a knife. He was hacking and swinging the knife at me, and I was beating him off with a lamp trying to block the knife. He ran out the front door and as I looked down at my neck I saw blood gushing out. He had cut my neck pretty bad.

I was losing a lot of blood. My dad ran and got a wet towel, and I applied pressure. He got me in the car and drove me to the ER Hospital there in Tamarac. They got me on a bed and in the ER room, and then a Cuban doctor sedated me and started stitching me up.

He asks if I was in the mafia or something? Then he said "O man if it had been 2 millimeters over more you would not made it to the Hospital. You would have died right there as that's a main artery." So in reality what the Doc was telling me was that I was 2 millimeters or a fraction of an inch from Hell. That was where my life of partying, drinking and drugging had taking me. God once again had his angels looking out for me and, for some reason, somehow someway He had my back.

I didn't want to press charges on the kid, and I knew I needed time to recuperate. I decided to ask the doc to send me to the Miami V.A. Hospital Alcohol Detox Ward. I told him I knew that I was messed up and I needed help. So they arranged to send me to the Miami V.A. Hospital. It was a world renowned hospital known for its success and high quality of drug and alcohol treatment. They had the best doctors, the best counselors, and the best psychologist available. It was an excellent program. But they couldn't fix me. This is where it became obvious that it was not an A.A. Program, or a V.A. Program that I needed. What I needed was beyond any program. I needed Jesus, and they did not have that on their little prescription pads.

Grandma Allie May Boyd reading the Bible

Uncle Johnny Boyd's Gravesite
Died of Alcoholism @ 51 years old

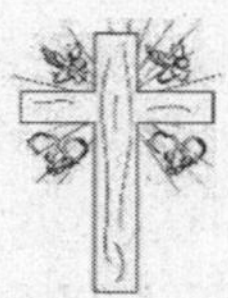

Chapter 8: New Orleans, The Darkness Gets Darker

After the fight and getting cut, my dad and I decided to take a trip out to Oregon and see his brother James Park. James and Betty Park had a small farm up in Woodburn, Oregon. In the past, my dad had spent time out there helping Uncle Jim with a small commercial salmon fishing business. I had never met them before, and I thought this would give me a chance to meet some of my dad's family, so I was game to take a trip out west.

We set off hitchhiking and heading that way. We made it through to Alabama and stayed around Bayou La Batrie partying for several days with some people we met while hitchhiking. Bayou La Batrie was a small shrimping and fishing town. Those folks worked hard and partied even harder. After we left Bayou La Batrie we made it to New Orleans. The party city of all time. Home of the famous French Quarter and Mardi Gras.

New Orleans was so different than Miami. This place was so different than any other place, and you could sense the spiritual fog and demonic darkness. The street people there were embedded into a small concentrated area of tourist around the famous French Quarter. There were a lot of junkies, wine-o's and drifters who if you could get them all together for a family photo it would have looked like some sort of zombie apocalypse.

The people down there spoke a different language and had an accent of their own, and they lived a different lifestyle. It was Creole and pure Louisiana accents that made me feel right at home with my Tennessee southern accent. This was a party city with hundreds of years of experience with the dark practice of drinking getting high and voodoo worship.

Living in the streets of New Orleans was a party with demons. Every night and day were consumed with hard drinking, hard drugs, and hard living. I sort of just let it consume me, and I became part of that inner city street people scene, homeless and hopeless, directionless and lost.

My dad and I got a few day labor jobs, while he waited for his V.A. check before we would try and move on toward Oregon. He got a little apartment, and we had street people in and out all the time partying, drinking, doing drugs and getting high. It was all day, all night, every day and every night and the demons of Hell raged in us out of control. The streets of New Orleans were hard core, and it was a sub culture of lost and hopeless souls. A place where mere survival meant getting a fix, a shot of dope, or a bottle of wine, whiskey or beer. It was a place of alcoholic psychosis and slowly drifting into a whole different realm of Satanic addiction and the bondage of Hell.

As it had been in the past, after a few weeks of being around my dad I would always get angry, and we would end up in a big hellacious fight. I felt deep resentment for having to grow up as a child without a dad. I never really had a father, because he abandoned me. He never showed up even after getting out of Prison in Tennessee. Deep inside I had a hatred toward him, and I hated that I had been forced to grow up without a dad to ever pitch a baseball with, or throw a football, or take me fishing, camping or hunting. I was stuck in some sort of love hate relationship with my dad that was all consumed by getting high and staying high.

In that apartment in New Orleans, we got in a fight, and I hit him and knocked him down the stairs. He was laying there knocked out cold at the bottom of the stairs and could have been dead for all I cared. I jumped over him and just ran out the front door.

I ran, and I ran down that street in New Orleans, but where was I running to in life? What was I running from and what was I running to? I had nothing to run to. I was a hopeless, homeless 22-year-old alcoholic drunk and drug addict. There was nowhere to run but to the streets. Into the deep darkness of addiction and sin I ran and I ran hard as I could. I wandered in the streets and back alleys of New Orleans for days. Sleeping in the weeds, passing out in the back alleys drinking with the wine-o's and junkies of the streets. I had made it to the gutters of sin, to the very gutters of humanity.

I remember walking down Camp Street some nights with a bottle of liquor and staggering and stumbling by the local rescue mission. I would step over men laying out on the sidewalk with their heads busted open, drunk and passed out, robbed and left like a stray dog. The Rescue Mission was a place to get a hot meal, a shower and a night of sleep, but it just never dawned on me that it was a place for rescue. I didn't think I needed to be rescued, what I needed was more whiskey, wine, dope, and beer. I didn't want or need Religion, what I needed was a good drink of whiskey and a hit of dope. Or so I thought.

Living on the streets is hard, living in bondage to Satan and Sin is hard. Every day was just another day of existence. You never think that you will go so deep or go so far as you end up. Like the old preacher shared one time, "sin will take you farther than you want to go and keep you longer than you want to stay. *"Woe unto them that call evil good, and good evil; that put* ***darkness*** *for light, and light for* ***darkness****; that put bitter for sweet, and sweet for bitter!" Isaiah 5:20.* Oh! How that truth of Scripture would come true in my sin shackled life.

How the drugs and the alcohol consumes you and you become a slave to the power that it has over you and your life is unimaginable. It is a bondage that is so strong as it is part of Satan's bondage. It drives you deeper and deeper into darkness and despair. Deeper and deeper into hopelessness, rejection and dejection.

New Orleans had a jail and before long I became a regular resident just like Otis on the Andy Griffith show. I was in and out numerous times for drunk and disorderly conduct. Picked up several times just passed out in a doorway or on a sidewalk. The Judge finally sentenced me to 30 days and sent me to the infamous "House of D." This was the main detention facility of New Orleans Parish.

Since I was just there for a short visit, they had me on small work details. I ended up working in the Property Room and painting and doing odd jobs for the officers that ran that department. They even took me out for a cold beer and got me a hamburger and fries occasionally. Good cops were trying to help a mixed up kid who had no clue where life was taking him.

Sometimes after hours, the jail would call for volunteers to do Morgue Duty. Some black kid in my cell told me, "come on man it's a lot of fun", and said that they would give us five bucks and a pack of cigarettes and he wanted me to go with him. Everyone else in the cell block was too scared. So why not, I needed some fresh air and extra cash.

It had been one of those heavy rain storms in New Orleans and they took us out in a small van that was used to recover bodies. When we got on the scene of our pickup, it was two teenagers who had drowned in the canal. We had to go down to the bank and get the bodies on a stretcher and carry them up to the van.

After we had got the bodies back to the Morgue we had to cut the clothes off and put any property in a little bag that they labeled and then we would wash the corpse off and put it on a slide into the Morgue's cooler. This was the first time I had ever experienced this side of death.

The reality of death. It was an entirely new experience to realize that this teenager was alive this morning and now here he was dead lying in a morgue. It all seemed so surreal and odd. But at the end of the shift, I just wanted my five bucks and the pack of cigarettes that I would later sell back at the jail cell since I didn't smoke. I would go out on several Morgue calls while in the House of D. It was sort of a pastime and something to make a few extra bucks. But it did illuminate to me that death was real, but that didn't seem to affect me in the least. Like most of us we always have that attitude Oh! That will never happen to me.

After getting released from the big "House of D," I decided I needed to move on. I needed to keep heading out to Oregon and visit my uncle Jim and his wife Betty. So I hit the highway once again, not sure where I was going or how I was going to get there. I was high and had a bottle of liquor and a good buzz going on, that was all that mattered.

Aunt Betty Park and Mickey @ the farm in Oregon

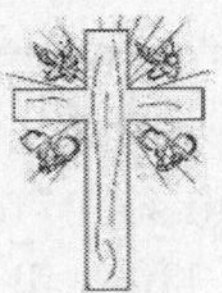

Chapter 9: The Texas Two-Step

Leaving New Orleans, I ended up after a few days in Dallas, Texas. It was a big city that sort of matched that saying everything's "Bigger in Texas." The street people in Dallas were not as well congested as in New Orleans, but it wasn't long before I found a few wine-o's and junkies to hang out with and get drunk with. The plan of the day was actually pretty simple. Get up, get drunk, pass out, and then get up and do it all over again the next day. Life was not complicated.

I was sitting on a bench in what was called Dealey Plaza. This is where they had the memorial of the President John F. Kennedy assassination. Dallas was the city where J. Harvey Oswald took his sniper shot and assassinated President John F. Kennedy. So they had this area as a memorial of that fateful event, and tourist and folks would come to visit and reflect.

As I was sitting there on a bench out of the way off to the side, high and drunk, sick and disgusting looking. I had ratty, dirty hair, dingy clothes; I had been drinking and drunk sleeping in the weeds and back alleys for days. I looked over at some men dressed in nice suits, and they were reading one of the memorial plaques, and it seemed like one of these guys I had seen before. To me he actually looked like a well known famous T.V. Preacher Evangelist but won't mention any names.

But I wasn't sure, and will never know for sure, as they just walked by me and on down the sidewalk to their car. But for me, that did seem to be so typical of most religious church folks. They all just walked by me, while I was lying there in the filth of sin. They just didn't want to get their hands dirty with the likes of me.

That is what religion and a lot of Church people do, is walk right by you, just like those Pharisees and Sadducees walked by that man on the Samaritan road. I don't blame them, I smelled like a wet dog and looked like a 22-year-old kid wasted on drugs and alcohol. It probably wouldn't have mattered anyhow; I didn't need or want their help, I needed another drink of whiskey and another hit of dope.

The days in Dallas were hard and harsh on me, and I began to realize that maybe I had better find a V.A. Hospital and see if they would take me in. I went down to Waco, Texas and checked into the V.A. Hospital's Alcohol and Drug recovery unit there in Waco. I thought maybe they could fix me; maybe they could help me overcome this life controlling confusion and addiction in my life.

The Waco V.A. was a large facility, and it had very good doctors and counselors and the best therapist in the area. Waco was also home to the famous Baylor University, and it had one of the best medical and psychiatric programs available. Many of the Doctors and Psychologist at the V.A. were from Baylor University. These were some of the best and brightest in the land. But all the King's horses and all the King's men could not put Mickey back together again.

Sorry ya'll, It wasn't Carl Jung or Sigmund Freud I needed, but it was JESUS. They couldn't help with that.

At the hospital, I met a patient there, and he was from Los Cruces, New Mexico, and as we got to be friends, he wanted me to come out and visit. He was a Mexican-American and had a strong alcohol problem, and like me was young and lost in the whirlwind of addiction.

My life was like that Texas Two Step, one step forward and one step backward. Backwards into the darkness and bondage of addiction. Backwards into the drugs and alcohol and one step forward to nowhere. One step forward to another high, another bottle of booze another joint of pot, another hit of dope. That was the life and the lifestyle I was trapped in.

We left the Waco V.A. and caught a bus to Los Cruces, New Mexico and once we got there we stayed around for a few days. We even went down to Mexico across the border and partied down there for a few days. I had always heard “don’t drink the water,” so no worry to me, I just drank all the beer and whiskey I could get my hands on. Mexico was just another party, just another high.

A dope addict and alcoholic in Mexico is the same as a dope addict and alcoholic on the streets of Miami, New Orleans, Dallas or Chattanooga, Tennessee. They may look different, speak an entirely different language but at the end of the day, they are all the same. Lost, hopeless and miserable without Christ and without direction.

There I sat shaking and trembling for another drink, jonesing and cringing for another hit of dope. Looking for some way to get another high.

Addiction is cruel and merciless. It does not care

about anything or nothing but keeping the flames of the fires of Hell burning in one's soul. Just like the pits of Hell, it is never satisfied. Here I was continuing to dance that two step, one step forward, and one step back. With no hope and no help in sight.

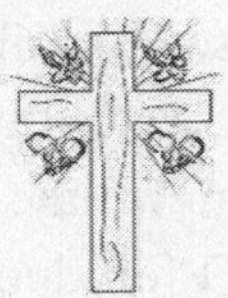

Chapter 10: Westward Ho! The Oregon Trail

Leaving New Mexico and heading on up to Oregon I began to wonder what that would be like. I did not really know Uncle Jim or his wife, Betty. I had no idea of what to expect or for what reason or even why I was going there. I had lost contact with my dad; I figured that he was still in New Orleans and that he would contact Jim and come on up eventually.

So I caught a bus and headed up to the Cascades of Oregon. Coming out of Nevada and then into those mountains of Oregon, it was so beautiful and majestic. It sort of reminded me of the mountains in Germany and the little Bavarian towns and villages in between each of the mountain ranges.

Somewhere along the way, the bus made a stop, and I got me a pint of whiskey to soothe my nerves as I was anxious about meeting these people I had never met before. The more I drank, the less it seemed to concern me. Unfortunately the more I drank, the drunker I got. That is just a basic law of physics. The one I had failed to consider. By the time the bus rolled into Salem, Oregon to the bus depot I was drunk, wild and crazy. Obviously not a good first impression on my new Park family. But then, after all, it was a "family tradition!"

They were for sure shocked to be picking up Mickey their nephew from Tennessee sloppy drunk and crazy out of his Tennessee hillbilly mind. But they took me home to Woodburn, to the farm and there I slept it off and got up to face a new day.

Needless to say, I felt deeply ashamed, and sincerely sorry but really didn't have any excuse or explanation. They were very forgiving and seemed that it was no big deal and just let it go.

It was very nice to have the fresh air of the farm and to be able to walk out and see Mt. Hood in the background with its snow peaks. It was so fresh and beautiful. My Aunt Betty was a very sweet and caring lady; she was still working as a meat wrapper at a local grocery store. Uncle Jim was a tall, husky guy that carried a flask of whiskey with him everywhere he went. So, needless to say, it was certainly love at first sight.

I helped Jim around the farm and was glad to be able to help him get a few odd jobs completed around there. They rented a large part of the land out to a local Strawberry farmer. They had their own cows, chickens, and a big garden. So I helped with whatever was needed.

Jim would tell me stories about my dad, his family and of their growing up in Chattanooga. It was so interesting since I had never really known much about my dad's side of the family. Jim shared about the hardships they had faced. How their dad was killed in a tragic accident on a motorcycle that collided with a train trolley in Chattanooga in the early 1930's. Leaving a family of 8 children fatherless. Then how in World War 2 they lost two brothers Thomas and Charles to combat.

Uncle Jim was also the oldest, and that seemed to put a lot of pressure on him to become the man of the house. It was a hard childhood, and it sort of made me appreciate what this Park family had been through.

Jim and Betty would drink every night, and Jim would always have his little flask of whiskey to take along with him. The epitome of a functional alcoholic is what that meant.

Certainly, not all alcoholics are on the streets or in the back alleys. Many work every day, and have a family but continue to lose out on so much of life running on empty and trying to fill a void and a vacuum in their lives with a bottle of booze.

My stay there with Jim and Betty was filled with the same old same old. As for me, I was still drinking but not quite as wild. I only got in a few bar room fights with some Russians in one of the local pubs. They had a lot of Russian immigrants in that area who had moved to America to farm and start a new life. After a few beers, I just had to pick a fight with some of them.

One night Jim and I were at the bar, and we were having this drunk talk conversation about Religion and God of all things. He was sharing how in the Army he was stationed at a camp in Oklahoma, as they would not allow him to go to war since the family had lost two sons already in the war. One night while pulling sentry duty he saw a bright light appear to him, and he really felt that the light was somehow the Lord trying to get his attention. So basically he married a good Catholic girl my Aunt Betty and had been Catholic ever since. He didn't say a good Catholic or if he had ever been saved or born again, just that he saw this light. I was sure not the one to be talking with about God, because I was just a demon infested drug addict alcoholic hillbilly hippie. I for sure could not help him in his quest for truth or to find that light; my life was all about darkness.

That night after we left the bar, we got back home to the farm I went upstairs to bed, and Jim went to bed. Several hours later I heard a horrific scream come from Aunt Betty down stairs, and I rushed down stairs, and she was out in the living room pointing to the bedroom all the while on the phone trying to call 911. I ran into the bedroom, and Jim had suffered a massive heart attack in his sleep. I tried to do CPR and resuscitate him until the ambulance got there, and they took him to the hospital, but it was too late. He was dead before they even left the house. He died in his sleep of a massive heart attack. All I knew then was I hoped that he found that light he was talking about.

After the funeral, I stayed around for a few weeks to help Aunt Betty get situated and as settled as she could. But I decided that I needed to go back to New Orleans and find Mack Mickle my dad and let him know his brother Jim was gone. I don't know a whole lot, but I do know that as for alcohol you can drink yourself to death, but you cannot drink yourself to life. Uncle Jim did not take his little flask of whiskey with him.

The bus dropped me off in New Orleans, and I was on a mission to find my dad somewhere in this dark demon infested city. I searched the streets and back alleys and asked around with some of the street people if anyone had seen him. No luck. So I kept searching. Sure enough, I stumbled upon him in a dark, dingy alleyway drunk and totally out of it. He was now homeless and living on the streets of New Orleans. I had a little money that Aunt Betty had given me, so we used that to get drunk together and spent a few days drinking and wandering around the city. I told him all about Uncle Jim and let him know as well that his sister Mary in Florida has suddenly died of some sort of drug complications, from what sounded to me like an overdose or heart failure. Both were now gone.

After a few days of New Orleans, I had decided to return home to Chattanooga and see my mother and try and maybe get back in school or something. It was time to go home again I was sick of the streets. I was tired, I was sick, and I was weary and so very much drained.

Mack Mickel and Jim Park

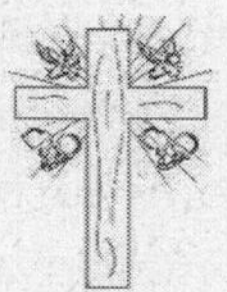

Chapter 11: The Tennessee Hills & Tennessee Whiskey

Getting back home to Chattanooga was always good for me. It was a good feeling to be back home. Everyone missed me and seemed glad to see me. At least they knew I was still alive and not dead in some back alley some place.

At first I stayed with my sister Linda and her husband down in Rossville, Georgia right across the State Line. I had re-enrolled to Chattanooga State Community college and had gotten a 2nd shift job at one of the Carpet Mills in Ringgold, Georgia. By now Mother had started back to drinking and was working on getting a divorce from my stepdad.

I was drinking a lot and was smoking pot and really had no interest in school. I got into a big fight with my sister and left from her house. A few days later I got drunk and decided to go over to her house and get my stuff, what little clothes I had left there. But everyone was gone when I got there, and the door was locked. No big deal I just took a big swig of beer and kicked the front door in. I kicked it totally off the hinges just like in the movies. It was totally rad. I got my stuff and took all the beer and whiskey they had and then left.

When they got home, they were not happy

campers at all. She even called the cops and took out a warrant for me to press charges and all. But by then I was up in Chattanooga and didn't care nonetheless. I figured she would get over it and sooner or later and just drop the charges. I just kept on drinking and partying and running wild. That was the life we lived, why not live it to the fullest.

Mother left my stepdad and came over to my little apartment I had rented up on Missionary Ridge in Chattanooga. A beautiful historic neighborhood with old Victorian Homes overlooking the beautiful City of Chattanooga. I had lied to the landlord and told him I was in College on the G.I. Bill and working two jobs. I was a non-drinker, non-smoker and had even thought about going to church some. Oddly enough he lived in the upstairs, and he was a Jehovah's Witness.

I tried to avoid him as much as I could and would duck and dodge him or hide when I saw him coming. I worked the 2nd shift job and did show up to class some days but not many. But one day when I was drunk, I crashed my car and ended up in the ditch by the landlord's house and I had to get a wrecker to get out of the ditch that sort of busted me. But he didn't fully understand how bad or how messed up I really was or that my alcoholic mother was living in the apartment and drinking quarts of Tennessee whiskey and smoking cartons of Cigarettes, and I was smoking bags of weed and had car loads of guys and girls over partying in his little dainty apartment. The poor guy was as clueless as a Jehovah's Witness could be.

The party life was going on hot and heavy, and everything seemed to be on cruise control for the most part. I had a little job, a little apartment, and was having full blown fun. It was all fun and games until one day I crashed mother's 1977 Monte Carlo head on into some other car coming over the Missionary Ridge. I was a horrible drunk driver and had already totaled over 21 cars and had over 20 DUI arrest. Make this number 22 and counting.

This was a bad day for me, the ambulance came and got me and put me in the back of the ambulance and I really didn't want to go to jail or to any hospital, so I started fighting the paramedics and trying to kick the doors open to make a run for it. But like that old Country Song, it always ends up, "I fought the Law, and the Law won!" They had to restrain me and used pepper spray but got me to the hospital. It was then when two big burly Hospital security guards had me handcuffed and the beat me senseless. They hit and punched me mercilessly and choked me all the while I was handcuffed and defenseless. The nurses did nothing to help they never said a word. It was like I was a piece of garbage and they didn't care.

After a few days at the hospital, it was then on over to Hamilton County Jail. That was the end of the road for me for a while, as they had me charged with so many charges I lost count. Then to make matters worse, some insurance attorney shows up, and I find out that they are suing my stepdad since he was the owner of my mother's car. I thought boy how stupid was that? He should have known better than to put it in his name knowing I would get a hold of it one day. Her car and the other folk's car were a total loss, just add it to my bill. My life was already a total loss.

In the Hamilton County Jail, I was not sure what was going to happen next. Then they come and told me they were going to extradite me to Walker County Georgia to face burglary and destruction of property charges for what I did at my sister's house. It was not looking good, and the future was looking bleak. Georgia prisons had plenty of open beds and I was headed for one.

They took me to the Walker County Jail and put me in a cell block downstairs. It was an old rusty jail, and actually, their claim to fame was that at one time Johnny Cash the great country music legend had been in this jail. The Sheriff even had a belt buckle on a plaque in his office from Johnny Cash himself. It was as country as country could get and here I was.

The guys in the cell were all cool, and just a bunch of drug addicts and wild country boys like me. They had the trustees smuggle in pot to us, and we would smoke dope and play cards and tell war stories of our days in the streets. There was not a lot else to do to pass the time, so the more entertainment, the better.

One time the trustee was able to smuggle in a pint of whiskey. So we really were living the High Life in the Jailhouse. We put a whole new meaning to that old Elvis song Jailhouse Rock.

As we were sipping our whiskey, one of the guys came up with a better plan. He had a syringe, and he figured we could just shoot up some hits of liquor, and it would last longer and give us double the buzz. So here we were shooting up rock gut liquor in a jail cell. How dark how demonic and disgusting is that. Lost and hell bound is what we were. I am not sure what Johnny Cash found in that Walker County Jail, but all I found was a way to get high.

I kept thinking that eventually my sister would come up and drop the charges. I was waiting and waiting. This was 1981, and President Reagan had gotten shot by the psycho boy John Hinckley. The world was crazy, and things were so weird. I gave up on thinking that she would drop the charges. I finally had my aunt Susie help get me out of it. She had helped me before, and so she helped me get out on bond.

Unfortunately, I did not have a car, and it was not likely I would get one. There were probably one group of people that hated me more than anything, and that was the used car salesman, especially the Buy Here, Pay Here guy. My way of doing things was buy here, don't pay here, I never paid a dime. I had mother sign for cars over and over, and I would drive it, wreck it, and total it and usually she had only paid one or two payments. So I was without a ride, but I was in luck because a nice deputy gave me a ride up to Chattanooga.

I got out of jail and stayed a few days over at my aunt's house and decided to call an old Army buddy in Houston, Texas. I asked him if I come for a short stay out his way. I needed to get out of town and get out fast, I was sure Hamilton County had warrants out on me. So what else was there for me to do but run baby run.

Here I was trying to run away from my problems and hope that they would somehow just magically disappear. My life was so full of pain, so full of hurt and confusion. That is where addiction will lead you. It will lead you into a dark dismal valley. A valley of hopelessness and despair. You can't really run away from your problems. Your problems will follow you and only get worse. In reality my problem was sin, I was a sinner in need of a Savior. I was running from the Lord's Love, Mercy and Grace, I was running from the very one that could truly help me. The Lord Jesus Christ.

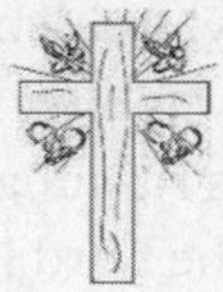

Chapter 12: Houston! We have a Problem!

Hitchhiking to Houston, Texas from Chattanooga was not that big of a deal. It was actually faster to hitchhike than hop a bus. Those bus routes have to stop in every small town and every major city to let folks off and pick up new people. So here I was running again, running from the law, from my home life, from my problems. I am not really sure what I was running from or running too. My head was so confused and mixed up. I couldn't make sense out of a clear day sober or drunk. I had let drugs and alcohol more or less take total control of my life. I was on some sort of internal autopilot and was just allowing the devils of hell to drive my life, direct my life and destroy my life.

Getting to Houston and having my Army buddy take me in was really a break from all the confusion and chaos of my wasted messed up life. Ishmael was a Mexican American, we had been stationed in Germany together. He was not a stoner or a drug user and only drank. He was a good man and a good friend. Maybe this was a chance for change, and I could get my life on track somehow. Regardless it was better than going to jail in Tennessee, so at least maybe this would be a new start.

Shortly after getting to Houston, I got a job. Of all

things as a security guard for a Rental Car Place at the Houston International Airport. Which was close to the apartment I was staying at. It was a cheesy job kind of like in the mall cop movie where you wore this fake cop uniform and drove around on a golf cart checking the car lot to make sure car doors were secure.

I also got to run the gate and check the cars out that were exiting the car lot. It was very non stressful and certainly non eventful. I got to know a few of the guys and girls working there. The shuttle bus girls were all cool and seemed nice; the car lot girls were all nice and friendly. Sometimes we would all go out to a bar together and would have some drinks. I learned that a few of them smoked weed and got high, so we all became party animals.

It wasn't long before we were partying hard and heavy with this new group of friends. All of us young and wild college age kids. One Mexican girl had gotten busted for possession of pot and some pills. She was now on probation. I tried to tell her not to sweat it just don't do anything too wild, and she'd be fine. Dude, I was sure not the best one to be giving anyone advice on how to stay out of trouble or stay out of jail. If they only knew all the warrants and jails I had been in and out of the past two years. I was an expert on getting in trouble and getting in jail, NOT an expert of staying out of trouble and staying out of jail.

The partying only got more and more intense. The entire group was just a bunch of kids who loved to drink hard and smoke dope. They were a great fit for me. I was in hog heaven now. I ended up moving out of my Army buddy's place and in as a roommate with two of the girls. We partied all the time, and I dated one of the other girls from the lot. It was crazy and wild.

The Rental car place had a system where if you worked there you could get a car to return to another City. They would sign out a car to return to New Orleans, and we would drive it over there, and party all the way and trash the car out really bad, then pick one up to drive back to Houston.

I got high and drunk one day and wanted to go to Galveston to the beach. So I had one of them give me the keys to brand new Ford EXP, which was a small sports car. I should have had better sense, after all remember I wrecked and total every car I ever had, plus ended up with a DUI 9 times out of 10. The odds were not looking good for that little Ford EXP.

Sure enough, when I got up on the Interstate in Houston, I was driving drunk and high out of my hillbilly mind. I side swiped some truck, then I slammed into the wall and finally ended up off the exit ramp at a stop light passed out at the wheel. The party's over. The next thing I knew was some big old Houston cop dragging me out of the front seat and dragging me to the backseat of his patrol car. All I remember is looking up at that pretty little red Ford EXP and seeing the fenders and doors hanging off of it. OOPS! That one is totaled.

At the Harris County Jail, things were not looking too good for me. The Rental car company had filed charges against me for felony unauthorized use of a motor vehicle. Which was sort of an understatement, but I couldn't really argue the issue of what defines authorized. Someone gave me the keys, even though they shouldn't have. That Harris County Jail system was so weird. It was like a fast food drive-through system. I had some guy from the probation office offering me a plea deal and probation release like the next day. He had me sign a few papers and told me to stay off drugs and alcohol, get a job and come see him in 5 days. I lied to him and promised him I would do the best I could. That I would be in Church on Sunday, if he let me out today.

I walked out of the Harris County Jail and went straight to the apartment and got my backpack of clothes, a six pack of beer, a bag of weed and the car keys to my Army buddy's old car he had been letting me drive. I was going to split town and get on the road. I thought maybe I needed to go to Canada and explore the North Country for a while. "Run baby run!"

So here I was running again, on the run and not sure what I was running from or where I was running too. Somehow in my doped up head, I thought probation meant you could just go run out of town and beat this. I had no intention of doing probation; it was not in my hillbilly ability to stay clean and drug-free long enough to do probation. What I also did not fully comprehend was that the only other option was Texas State Prison. That was even more of a reason to hit the road Jack and never come back no more, no more.

The poor old car that I stole from my Army buddy only made it to the Colorado-Utah State Line. The tire went flat, and the spare was shot, and I had picked up a bunch of hitchhikers, and we were all on a Colorado Mountain High, so we drove the car on its rim because we were miles and miles from a gas station. It wasn't like I could have just called AAA, so we drove the old car until it would drive no more. Then I ditched it and started hitchhiking, heading north toward the Canadian border.

That abandoned busted up car was just a representation of my life. Like it, I was broken, busted and damaged beyond repair. Ready for the junk yard of life. The choices I had made were going to deliver some harsh and hard consequences. But addiction and sin will deceive you to follow a path of life that will only get worse. Your dreams become nightmares, your successes become failures. Life becomes a living nightmare for which you had never planned for.

Chapter 13: A Canada High

I was in Utah and still trying to get my bearings on what to do and where to go. It was an amazing time to see some of the most awesome beauty out West. I went through Mt. Zion National Park, then to Arches National Park and I camped out and planned out where to go next. In a sense, I felt like a real outlaw. Like the old Wild Wild West days, here I was on the run from the Texas Rangers. I really just wanted to backpack through Canada and get high, and stay stoned. All I wanted to do was enjoy that free spirit and extend my freedom. Or at least enjoy the freedom I had while I had it. I knew I would probably be going to Texas Prison for 2 to 3 years. I knew that I had really blown it out of the water this time with the Ford EXP ordeal. It was a violation of felony probation, and they were not going to be giving me any breaks this time. So keep on running. Roll another joint, take another hit.

I hitchhiked on up through Idaho and was walking off the interstate by a motel when I saw some guy leave his luggage out in the front. I guess he went to get his car or forgot something back in the motel. I grabbed the suitcase and ran to the back of the motel and made it to the woods where I got the suitcase open and hallelujah there was some cash and a lot of traveler's checks. I would use these stolen checks all through Canada and enjoy the free ride.

Waking up in Banff Canada with a backpack, a six pack and a pint of whiskey was like living a dream for this hillbilly junkie. It was one of the most beautiful places I had ever encountered. The rivers and mountains were majestic, with snow peaks and lush green trees. I was ready to enjoy this place to the fullest. Now, all I needed was some pot to smoke and a cold beer to drink.

Once in the city area, it was easy to find some street people who were willing to help me get some weed, tell me how to avoid the police and Canadian Mounties and how to survive. It was a different atmosphere. It reminded me of my days in Germany. Here I was in an entirely different country living on the streets homeless and hopeless. Running from my past failures but not really running to anything or anywhere just running. Here I was drifting aimlessly with the wind of life, and not sure where I would end up.

There was a big drugie subculture in Canada and they sort of just wandered around shooting dope, smoking dope and popping pills. They were like me aimless and directionless. Sort of like a bunch of doped up zombies. So I fit in real good with the dope addicts and alcoholics there in Canada. It was just a normal way of life. Every day was a new day to get up, get high, get drunk, and get on with it. *"Keep Calm and Party on."*

Like them, I had nothing else to live for and nothing to die for. I was lost and lonely and drifting with the wind. Wherever it would blow me, I would just go. There was no rhyme or reason to my life.

In Banff, I met another dope addict alcoholic homie to run with. He had been to prison in Canada, and he knew how to run prescription fraud schemes, get prescription pads from Doctors' Offices and get dope. I was all in. Let's see how HIGH a Canadian high can go.

It was there that I started shooting synthetic heroin, T's & Blues and some cuts of heroin. It was there that I began to use needles. I used to say that will never happen to me. I will never be an IV drug user, or a useless junkie. Now here I was shooting dope with some dope fiend from Canada. Sin will take you further than you want to go and keep you longer than you want to stay. I used to say that will never happen to me, but there it was happening to me and in a bad way.

We ended up stealing a car, a big 1981 Mercury Grand Marquis so my new dope partner and I could ride high. We had the dope man car. We hit every major city in Central and Western Canada. Running prescription pads, shooting dope, smoking dope and drinking hard whiskey from one end of the country to the other. We went to Calgary, then up to Edmonton, then back down to Banff, then over to Vancouver chasing that high life yet running on empty.

Vancouver was to me like Amsterdam. It was a druggie mecca. The street people there were hardcore street hippies and drug addicts. They were like professional drug addicts and had somehow made it seem legal and legit and even cool to be like them. The abnormal was the normal to those folks.

The big problem with drug addiction is that you never really get enough. It is a demonic bondage that just keeps growing and growing until in the end it totally consumes you. Addiction is merciless and has no compassion. It only takes more and more of one's life and it is like Hell itself, it is never full and never fully satisfied.

While in Vancouver I decided why not head south and go to Oregon and see Aunt Betty, my Uncle Jim's widow. Then I would head on down to Texas and see if we could party with the folks back in Houston.

As crazy as it might seem we were actually able to drive that stolen Mercury across the border and into the United States. Here I was living off of stolen credit cards, dope money and any cash we had stolen from cars and motel rooms along the way.

I made it to Oregon and stopped in to say hey to Aunt Betty. I lied to her and told her we were working on a job in Texas and were on our way back. We pressed on through and headed to California and just kept partying on. Most of the time the Canadian ex-con, dope partner I was with was driving, and it was in Phoenix Arizona where his luck eventually ran out.

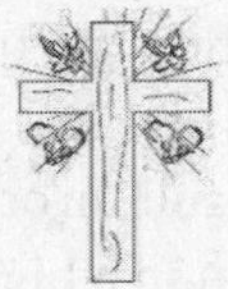

Chapter 14: I'll be in Jail for Christmas

Shooting drugs, smoking pot, drinking whiskey all while riding high in a big Mercury Grand Marquis is stuff you only see in Hollywood movies, not a normal reality for sure. The Canadian dope partner had been doing most of the driving, and that was good considering my history of DUI and Hit and Runs. Unfortunately, the luck ran out for him in Phoenix Arizona when the Arizona Highway Patrol pulled him over and did a sobriety test. They took him to Maricopa County Jail for DUI. They left me the car and left me to sleep it off. Those crazy cops did not do a very good background check on me. They really should not have left me with a big stolen hot Mercury Grand Marquis and a trunk full of liquor? That was not a good mix. Sort of like gasoline and fire. Something is for sure going to blow up.

I left the city of Phoenix and hit I-10 heading for Texas without the dope partner home boy. Which he probably was going to be stalled for a few months anyhow. I just wanted to keep moving and get to Texas. The more I drank, the wilder I got. Before long I was going 95 and 100 mph flying down I-10 like I was invisible. Flying High.

Sometimes when driving and getting high, I would get drunk and mean and play a little game. I would see some dude hitchhiking on the side of the Interstate and pull over and pop the big trunk latch so he could throw his backpack and gear in. Then once he shut the trunk, I would drive off full throttle burning rubber and spinning out leaving him in a big cloud of dust yelling and waving his arms chasing after me... Bye! Bye! See ya!

It was all fun and games until I almost got to the New Mexico State line, and the Arizona Highway Patrol got behind me, hit the blue lights and chased me over the State Line into New Mexico. The game was for sure over, and they took me to a little county jail there in New Mexico, and they extradited me and took me back to the Cochise County Jail in Bisbee, Arizona. I found out that this was the area of Tombstone Arizona where the O.K. Corral shoot out happened, and was where all the cowboy outlaws roamed.

Now here I was and my outlaw days were over. They charged me with a bucket list of charges like fleeing and eluding a police officer, reckless driving, reckless endangerment and of course DUI. The party was over.

Christmas day came, and I was stuck in the Cochise County Jail waiting on extradition to Houston, Texas and the Harris County Jail. This was my 1st Christmas I had ever been in jail. I had been in a lot of jails in a lot of places just never over Christmas. I had always been able to get out, but not this time. There was no getting out of jail this time, and it looked like I would be going to the Texas State Prison system at the end of the line. I was sure I was going to Texas State Prison.

The end of the party had come to a full circle. Now I would go to Texas and face the judge and hoped whatever happened would work out the best it could. Maybe 2 to 3 years.

The next stop of 1982 would be Harris County Jail, Houston, Texas. The Texas Rangers or whatever they were from Harris County Texas flew out to Tucson, Arizona and got me from the Cochise County Jail and flew me back to Houston and delivered me to the Harris County Jail. This jail system was big and ominous just like Miami-Dade County Jail. It was bad, and it was a tough place be. The inmates ran the cell barracks, they had what they called Barrack Trustees, and they would beat dudes up, bloody them up and then throw them in the shower wash them off and start all over. That was like their recreation. I saw guys come in and the next day have black eyes, or a tooth knocked out. It was a rough jail and just a precursor for the rough prisons of Texas. A few years later the Federal Government Justice Department came in and intervened in the Harris County jail system as it was one of the most brutal and mismanaged and corrupt jails in the Nation.

It was not a fun place, and I just knew I had to survive and stand up because I knew that I would be going down the road to Huntsville to the state prison system. I was so sick to think that was my next stop. I would talk to dudes who had come back for trial, and they had horror stories of the farms and the hard labor that the Prisons forced inmates to do. Texas in the 1980's was not a soft prison system, and it was well known as one of the worst.

I would play cards, or play chess with guys and talk to dudes that had 40 years to Life, or who had a Life Sentence for Robbery and Murder which they had gotten involved in while high on drugs. It seemed unfathomable to me that these men would be sentenced to 20, 30, 40,

99 years to Life. As I got to know them I felt so sorry for them, and it made me sick to think what they had to face. I would say to myself "That will Never Happen to Me!" I am not going down that road. I kept telling myself that as if to convince myself to make it true.

My life was a hot mess. I had some Mexican dude put some jail house tattoos on me. I think I gave him a couple packs of cigarettes and a soup for a playboy bunny, a big marijuana leaf and a Mickey Mouse giving the finger to the world. That sort of summed up my attitude and philosophy of life. It was mostly just to kill the time and break up the monotony of captivity. I had told myself I would never get a tattoo, just like I had told myself I would never shoot dope. Moral of the lesson is to be careful what you say you will never do.

Things were for sure looking bleak for me. The court appointed attorney was useless, and I could tell my case was just a rubber stamp to him. I decided I needed to come up with an option B plan. So I hit the law library and had some of the jailhouse lawyers point me to the law books and to some case law that would maybe save my sinking ship.

I was desperate, and I was so mixed up. What a big mess I had made of my life. I was in trouble and deep trouble at that. I was not religious and for sure had not been looking to God or Jesus for a bailout this time. I was so confused. I could read the Bible, and not one thing made any real sense to me. But I did pray, and I did ask God to please help me. You know that jailhouse religion prayer where you call out to God begging him to help you get out of this hot mess you got yourself into. I didn't hear any voices from Heaven, but I did believe that if anyone could help me out of this mess, it was God and God alone.

The jailhouse lawyers and the law books came up with one obscure Texas case law that related to the unauthorized use of a motor vehicle to where it could be reduced from a 3rd degree Felony to a Misdemeanor. That was the only chance I had. On the day of my court appearance, and on a hope and a prayer I gave the papers to the attorney and asked him to present it to the Judge. He was skeptical but willing to try it.

The attorney went in and laid it out to the Judge and to my amazement the Judge agreed to reduce it from a Felony to a Misdemeanor. So with time served for the rental car ordeal, I was able to walk out of the Harris County Jail, Houston, Texas in April 1982 and once again see how there is a God of 2nd chances. It wasn't the Easter Bunny looking out for me; it was for real JESUS CHRIST.

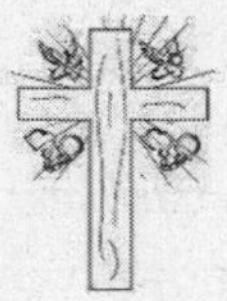

Chapter 15: Chattanooga Choo Choo

Walking out of Harris County Jail after facing Prison time in Texas would have been a wakeup call for most people. For a lot of people, it would have been an opportunity to pick up the pieces of a busted up life and start living for God and to straighten up. Few people get to experience the Grace and Mercy of a Holy God with a 2nd Chance like I had just received. It was for sure a real miracle and something to be so grateful for.

How would I show my gratitude?

My mother sent me a money order to catch a bus from Houston to Chattanooga. I cashed that money order and went straight to the liquor store and got a quart of beer and pint of Tennessee Whiskey. It was time to celebrate and get the party on. That makes me think of that old song, "Pardon me boy, is that the Chattanooga Choo Choo," that is exactly what I did. I just let the train of God's grace pass me by. I missed that train big time and walked back into the darkness of demonic addiction and was sloppy drunk and out of my head by the time I got to Huntsville, Alabama on my way to Chattanooga.

Getting home and to my mother's place it was so good to breathe fresh air. She was divorcing my stepdad and had a shack-up boyfriend who was the Road Commissioner of one of the little Tennessee cities around Chattanooga. She was back to drinking and was ready to party. We drank and drank and stayed drunk at the house in Georgia for days into weeks. It all became a big blur.

I got back in school just to draw a V.A. check, and I was able to get her to go to one of those used car dealers, the good old "Buy Here Pay Here" dealers to get me a little car. I was drinking and smoking a lot of weed. It wasn't long before that Chattanooga Choo Choo wild lifestyle would train wreck again.

I was pulling out of a bar about midnight one night and hit another car. I was drunk and just took off and kept going. It was a few days later that a Catoosa County Georgia Sheriff's Deputy was knocking on the door and asking where Mickey was. I hid in the back closet while mother told him I was not there. He knew good and well that I was back there hiding somewhere, the banged up car was parked in the garage. But Mother held her ground and told him Mickey's not here and no you can't come in and slammed the door in his face.

He told her that they had warrants on me for hit and run in Chattanooga and he needed to talk to me to get it resolved. Then he left. I knew that I needed to catch out of town as fast as I could. I knew that they would be coming back with a search warrant and they would be taking me to jail. I had to get out of there and run, "run baby run," but where to run to? I wasn't sure, but I knew I was running somewhere. The only place that came to my mind was Miami, I could go down there to see if I could by chance find my dad. Find Mack Mickle Park.

I stole my mother's boyfriend's credit cards; I didn't like him anyway. Then, I hit the highway, high and wild and on my way to Miami to see if I could find my dad Mack Mickle. I knew he was homeless living on the streets of Miami and I was gonna find him. How crazy was that? With Miami a city of 5 million people, I just knew I would find Mack Mickle drinking some George Dickel somewhere on the streets of Miami.

The ragged out car was an old Ford Pinto and still had the temporary dealer tag in the back window. The front end was all banged and busted up from the hit and run in Chattanooga. It had duct tape holding the left headlight in place and a bungee strap holding the hood down. But the drunker I got the better it drove. Most important of all it had a good tape player and a lot of good old Rock N Roll cassette tapes. So the Party was on. Miami here I come. The Chattanooga Choo Choo on a buzzed ride. Heading for a train wreck.

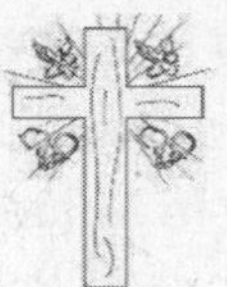

Chapter 16: Mack Mickle George Dickel and the Last Dance

Somehow I made it to Miami drunk wild and crazy. Sort of normal for me. I had stopped by Jacksonville to visit an old Army buddy. Freddy was a dope smoking wild rock-n-roller. He played the guitar like Jimi Hendrix who was one of his idols. We rolled a few buds and had a few laughs, and I headed on out of Jacksonville going to Miami.

I had picked up a few hitchhikers and let them do most of the driving. However, now it was just me, and I needed to find my dad, Mack Mickle Park. He was a homeless U.S. Marine Korean War Veteran. Miami had 5,000 to 10,000 homeless people living in the streets in 1982. This was back when they had their own tent cities and had overtaken I-95 overpasses and turned them into homeless condos of tents and tarp lean-to tents. What would be the odds of finding someone in a City of 5 million people? It was like trying to find a needle in a haystack, and this was a big haystack.

I drove all around the homeless areas, I got out and walked around and asked some of the street people if they knew of him. It was not looking good. I decided to stop by the Miami-Dade County Library off Biscayne

Blvd. and look around. One time before I had found my dad homeless on the streets of New Orleans and I just knew I could find him in Miami, but just not sure where. All of a sudden in a grove of Palm Trees off the sidewalk I saw him sitting on the grass.

He was shocked that I had found him. So was I for that matter. I told him I had a cooler of cold beer and a 5th of good Tennessee Whiskey in the car. Let's go party. He was all game for that. So the party was on. I took off for Key West. I wanted to watch the sun set in Margaretville and hit the beach and play in the sand in Key West.

The drive down to Key West was wild and crazy. I stopped and picked up some dude that was hitchhiking down that way. He had some pot, so now we had all the ingredients for a wild and crazy party night. We made it to the Florida Keys, we drank and smoked dope and passed out in the car and the next day got started back to Miami.

With the hitchhiker driving, the rock music blaring, and the pot smoke billowing we were screaming like demons and living that demonic destructive lifestyle. As we came up I-95 on the way back to Miami, I started getting wild and mean. I felt those feelings of hate and resentment to well up against my dad. I started cussing him out and telling how he had destroyed my childhood and messed my entire life up. How I hated him, and he was no good. We started fighting, and I was trying to hit him with a tire iron, and he was trying to hit me with a beer bottle.

The guy stopped the car, and we both jumped out, and we were still swinging fist and the tire iron and fighting. My dad ran down the Interstate 95 and got away. I had no idea then that would be the last time I would ever see my dad again.

I got back in the car, and the guy drove off on up I-95 north. We continued to drink and smoke weed, and I said let's go to New Orleans and keep the party going. I had been drinking hard for about four weeks straight non-stop, and it was starting to get to me. Plus the argument with my dad was very draining. My life was just a life full of the confusion and destruction of addiction. It was dark, dismal and hopeless even on a sunny Florida day.

As we got close to Ft. Lauderdale, a Florida Highway Patrol car pulled behind us and hit the blue lights. I started stashing the dope and hiding the beer bottles. Then I looked over at the Hitchhiker dude who was driving, and all I knew it was not going to end well for him. He was drunk, and he was driving and not me. I said to myself under my breath "bye, bye."

The Highway Patrol officer took him to jail, and they had the car towed in. That left me with a backpack, a six pack, and little bag of weed. So I decide to keep pressing on toward New Orleans. I thought maybe I would get to Gulfport Mississippi and check into a V.A. Hospital. I was caught up in a demonic darkness and could not find any light in my darkness. I was sick, tired and hungover from the hangovers.

After hard drinking for so long and smoking dope for so long, I was becoming detached from any reality. My hands were shaking and trembling for a drink; I was jonesing for a shot of dope. The demons of hell were driving the bus not me. I was on a Highway to Hell, and it was more than just a good old Rock-N-Roll song. It was like I was shackled and chained to a demonic power controlling my life and my life was totally out of control.

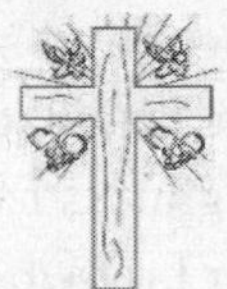

Chapter 17: The Darkest Day of My Life

Sitting there on I-95 as the wrecker came to tow the car, I had thought about jumping the wrecker driver and taking the car. I was so mixed up and confused. I decided that would only land me in the Broward County Jail, so I let him take the car. Then I went into the woods off the Interstate and passed out.

The next day I crawled out of the gutters off the highway and got on Interstate 95 North and headed up the road. I was able to get about halfway up to the middle of the state and then cut over to the west coast side and ended up on Highway US 98.

All I had was a backpack with some dingy, dirty clothes, a few beers and a life full of nothing but emptiness and pain. Addiction doesn't care, and it has no compassion, it digs deeper and deeper into the lost, hopeless soul to torment it more and more. It was a hot August day, and I was sick and sweating, tired and hungry.

I was on U.S. 98 in the little beach community of Destin, Florida. I stashed my backpack in the woods and went into a little store off the highway there and stole some cold beer and some sandwich meat and hotdogs. I stuck the six pack and meat in a grocery sack to look like I had already checked out and walked out unnoticed.

With the cold beer and some food to eat, I headed down toward the water to find a secluded place to rest and crash for the night. As I walked down through the woods, I saw another boy who was sitting over by the water, and I took a double look. He was sitting there smoking a joint of pot. Yeah baby, just what the doctor ordered! I went up to this dude and said "hey man, you want a cold beer?" He said "sure! Do you want a toke" and hands me the joint?

We sat there for a few hours drinking my beer and smoking his dope. We were like best bro's, and I didn't know this dude from Adam. He was stoned, and I was stoned, and we just kept drinking and smoking. I made another beer run up to the store, and we spent that day and the next day just partying and getting high.

The drunker we got, and the higher we got he began to tell me he knew a man close by that we could rob and get some fast cash. As we got drunker and drunker, he talked about killing the man, and how he hated him. I thought in my mind that was just all drunk talk dude, let's just steal the cash and credit cards and go to New Orleans and party hardy.

As it got dark, we continued to talk about going over to this place and robbing this guy. We decided to call on the Demons of darkness and seek the powers of Satan to empower us. In the midst of all the booze and all the pot smoke, we sat there chanting incantations to Satan. The darkness just got darker.

We went to the apartment, and he started up the stairs and as I started to go up the steps I felt a voice speak to me saying, "Mickey don't go." Now, I believe it was God trying to stop me from going up those stairs, but in my drunken crazed mind I just brushed it off and went on up.

The boy I was with knew this man, and he let us in thinking we wanted to drink and hang out. Once in the apartment, we had the music blaring, and we were drinking and waiting for the next move. The dude hit the guy, and I jumped him from behind and started choking him and knocked him out unconscious.

While he was knocked out on the living room floor, I went into the kitchen and was getting a beer out of the refrigerator, and was going to start looking for the car keys, the credit cards, and cash. While I stood there in the kitchen, I saw the dude I was with come around me and go into the kitchen drawer. Then he ran out back into the living room. I staggered back to the living room and stood there in a state of shock, as the dude had taken a butcher knife out of the kitchen and was standing over the man cutting his throat. You could feel the very presence of evil that night, and we were part of it. This is where partying with the demons of Hell had gotten me. The entire atmosphere was satanic, dark, demonic and hideous.

This was no longer just a simple, strong armed robbery, this was now a murder, and I was part of it, it was no longer fun and games, this was the power and influence of Hell real and up close. This is where addiction and that party hardy demonic lifestyle had ended up for me. In a panic, we loaded the body up in the car and took off to dispose of it. Then the other boy jumped out of the car and left me. I ended up disposing of the body in some woods and taking the car to Tennessee.

I was so drunk and so high, so scared, mixed up and confused. I thought I would get to Tennessee and get with my Mother and we could ditch the car and just cover it all up. I drove to Chattanooga and when I got home I found out mother was in a hospital detox center for Alcoholism.

It was while driving out to the hospital when a Hamilton County Tennessee Sheriff's car pulled behind me and hit the blue lights. I sped off, trying to outrun them and made it to the Interstate, where now it was 3 or 4 police cars chasing me down I-75 south. I had a cold beer in my hand and was cursing the cops and giving them the finger when they pulled up beside the car and motioned to pull over.

Right across the Georgia State Line they ended up doing a pit maneuver and bumped me into the guardrail. They then drug me out of the front seat of the car and threw me in the backseat of a Catoosa County Sheriff's patrol car and took me to the Catoosa County jail. This was the first jail I got put into at 17 for DUI, drunk and disorderly conduct; now here I was locked in a solitary confinement cell charged with 1st Degree Murder and Robbery in the State of Florida.

The next day I had drug and alcohol withdrawals so bad that the jailers would bring little styrofoam cups of whiskey back to me to keep me from going into full blown "alcoholic DT's." That morning when I looked out the cell door, the prisoners in the other cell pod looked over at me and asked "hey are you Mickey Park?" I said "yes," and they said "man, they just had you on the radio news on Rock 104, you're wanted in Florida for Murder and Mutilation." I sat down on that jail bed and realized I had wasted my life that I had gotten involved in something that was so awful and I felt so deeply ashamed and disgusted about where I had let my life go.

The prisoner in the next cell was a guy I used to get high with and smoke pot with and he called over the bars and said "Mickey, dude Florida has the Death Penalty."

After a few days, the Sheriff even sent a preacher back to the cell. He came up and said "son the Sheriff explained that you're in a lot of trouble. Would you like me to pray with you?" I got up from that jail bed and walked up to the bars and told him, "Preacher I don't need Prayer, what I need is a shot of dope and drink of Whiskey!" He left a few gospel tracts on the cell and walked away shaking his head. I gathered up those gospel tracts and went over to the toilet, and I flushed those tracts down the commode. I was so bitter, and I was full of hate and hurt. I hated God, I hated my life, and I hated what I had done.

The jailers would come back and tell me that girls and teachers had called from Chattanooga State Community College saying that they knew me and that it could not be the Mickey they knew. I was so disgusted with my life. It was like a bad dream, like some nightmare. I had let drugs and alcohol and my bad choices totally wreck and ruin my life and even cost the life of another.

This was not what I had planned or expected or hoped for in my life. No one gets up one day and says

"Oh! I think I will go to jail for the rest of my life today."

The progression of Sin is sever and devastating. What started out as a teenager just partying, drinking, getting high and running wild ended in a dark horrible nightmare.

That night of the crime was the darkest day of my life, and I will regret it for the rest of my life.

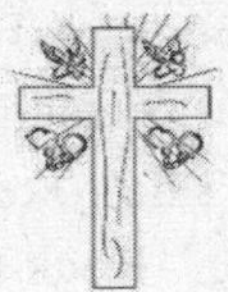

Chapter 18: From Rock Bottom to The Rock of Calvary

The Okaloosa County Sheriff's Deputies came in a few days and took me back to Florida and straight to the Okaloosa County Jail. There would be no get-out-of-jail card this time. They placed me in a solitary confinement cell and separated me from the other boy. He had been captured and of course told them I did it not him. The local law knew him well and knew that he was a friend to the victim. They knew we would try and kill each other if we got the chance, so they put me in solitary confinement.

There I sat in a solitary confinement cell, busted, disgusted and all alone. I had no money for an attorney; I had no family that could help me. My dad was homeless on the streets of Miami, my mother in an alcoholic detox hospital up in Tennessee. I had nothing and no one. It was a hopeless and a dismal situation. I had hit rock bottom, and I mean hit it hard. My life had no meaning, no purpose and I felt that I was a useless piece of trash.

After a few weeks in jail, a Bailiff from Okaloosa County Court came by the cell and asked are you Mickey Park? And then handed me some papers and said, "the

Okaloosa County Grand Jury has indicted you for 1st Degree Murder and Robbery" Then as he walked away he stopped and turned and sneeringly said, "Oh! and the State Attorney's Office said to tell you they do intend to seek the "Death Penalty." Rock Bottom just got a little deeper for me.

It was after that ordeal that the weight of sin and the burden of hopelessness really began to take its toll on me. The satanic voices of Hell begin to whisper in my mind, that suicide would be my best option. That I didn't have to face this overwhelming pain. I should just kill myself and be done with it.

I began to think, you know I have enjoyed a full life, I have fished and hunted in the hills of Tennessee, and I have been to Germany, to the Swiss Alps and enjoyed the Canadian Rockies and beautiful mountains and rivers. Why rot in prison for life or sit the rest of my life on death row? I could just check out and be done with all this mess, and hope that death would kill the pain of living and end this awful nightmare that I was in.

The plan was to hang myself, and I watched the guards, how and when they usually made their rounds. I was in a dark, cold and lonely solitary confinement cell way in the back hall of the Jail; no one came around other than a routine check. The more I thought about it, the more I could sense the demons of Hell becoming stronger and saying to my soul "yes, yes, yes do it, go ahead and do it." You could sense the very presence of evil in that cell. That same spirit that was in the apartment that night, that eerie feeling of a dark demonic and satanic presence.

I had tied some sheets together and was watching

for the guard to make their rounds. I was all alone and had nothing and no one, empty and hopeless in a dark, dingy jail cell. I was going to go through with it and right as I made my mind up and got the nerve pumped up, I heard a soft still voice speak to my desperate hurting heart, "Mickey, why don't you Pray? Just out of respect for Grandma," I remembered that my Grandma, Allie May Boyd who had been the only Christian influence in my life, and how she had died that day in the hospital with a prayer.

I got down on my knees just out of respect for my grandmother. I knelt by that hard steel jail cell bed on that dirty, dingy jail cell floor, and I prayed, "Dear God, if you are real and I do believe you are Lord, please Save me or just let me die." It was then that the tears began to flow from the inner depths of my broken heart and soul.

I laid there on that filthy jail cell floor and cried and cried as I asked the Lord Jesus Christ to forgive me and to save me and change my life. To forgive me not only for the crime that I was in jail for, but for my entire life of sin, my whole lifestyle of rebellion and rejection of His love.

That night this rebel met the Redeemer, and the Glorious light of the Gospel of Jesus Christ shined into the darkness of that dismal jail cell and into the darkness of my life. What was dark and demonic just moments before now had the light of glory beaming in. My life was in His hands, and I felt for the first time in my 25 years of living the real Love of a loving Father. The Lord Jesus Christ reached down with his nail scarred hands and picked me up out of the gutter of sin.

Ps. 40:1-3 I waited patiently for the Lord; and he

inclined unto me, and heard my cry. He brought me up also out of a horrible pit, out of the miry clay, and set my feet upon a rock, and established my goings. And he hath put a new song in my mouth, even praise unto our God: many shall see it, and fear, and shall trust in the Lord.

"That night in that jail cell I went from Rock Bottom to the Rock of Calvary!"

.

Yes, the Consequences of Sin are real. After I got up from praying that night and asking the Lord to save and change me everything was different. I knew I had been touched and that the Lord had entered into my heart and life in a real way. But the jailers didn't come down the hall that next morning with the keys and open the cell door and say "O.K. Mickey, you've accepted Jesus now you can go home!" No, it doesn't work like that. You see there are consequences to sin and to the poor choices we make. I still had to face the charges of the crime I had committed, I was still facing the possibility of going to Florida Death Row or at best spending the rest of my life incarcerated. All that was still a very harsh reality, but now I had the Lord Jesus Christ to help me walk in His Grace and to sustain me in my desperate time of need.

"The Lord was so real to me, it was like I was A newborn baby!"

A newborn baby that had a light in my Heart and Joy in my soul. It was then I understood what Christians meant by referring to being "Born Again." I felt that fullness of God's Grace in my life and I felt that freedom from the past shackles of sin and degradation. ***John 8:36 If the Son therefore shall make you free, ye shall be free indeed. Praise God! I had found FREEDOM in a jail cell. The shackles and chains of my past were broken, they were gone. I WAS SET FREE!***

There was a jail ministry volunteer Chaplain named Brother Dennis who would come around who was an ex-drug dealer and had a real love for the Lord. He had a ministry there at the jail and had his family who would come in and sing and share in the Saturday night chapel services held in the chow hall. But because I was still in isolation and solitary confinement I could not attend. So Chaplain Dennis began to mentor me and come to the jail during the week and have one on one Bible study time with me and counsel me and encourage me. He took a lot of time and extra effort to help me grow in my new found faith in Christ and helped me learn to read and study the Bible. I will forever be grateful for Chaplain Dennis as he allowed God to use him. He was not perfect, but was one brother who had found Jesus and was trying to pass the light of Christ on to another and he sure helped me.

I wrote my mother in Tennessee and shared with her what had happened and how sorry I was for where my life had ended up but that I had a real relationship with Christ now and my heart's desire was to live and grow in him. She mailed me my study Bible that she had bought me right after I came home from the

Army. It was that Thompson Chain Reference Study Bible and even had my name engraved on it and the date she had given it to me was written in it - "1979".

Oh! Only if I would have applied that Bible and the word of God to my life then, I would not have been sitting in that jail cell facing the possibility of death row in September 1982. The more I studied that Bible, the more on fire I got for the Lord. I was witnessing to men in the cells and leading men to accept Christ and praying with them. I was testifying and sharing how God can deliver and set us free from the bondage of drugs, alcohol, and sin. How God had worked a miracle of change in my life, and He could do it in theirs as well.

I spent day and night reading the Bible and praying and growing in the Lord. Reaching deep for His truth and His living promises to apply to my heart and life. Chaplain Dennis continued to do Bible Studies with me and edified and encouraged me to seek God and grow in my love for Christ. That love and passion continued to grow and glow in the Love, Mercy, and Grace of Jesus Christ.

By October the jail staff finally saw that I was a changed man and they moved me out of solitary confinement into a general population cell. Which Hallelujah! Glory to God! That meant I could go to the Chapel services now with Chaplain Dennis. Those services were so awesome, so refreshing and rejuvenating spiritually. The Lord was working in a mighty way.

One night as I was laying in my bunk and praying and reading my bible I felt God speak to my heart, that He was calling me to the ministry and wanted me to become a preacher of the Gospel of Jesus Christ so that I could tell others what great things God has done. I was overwhelmed at the thought of me being a preacher, I had no Bible College Education and had failed Public Speaking in Community College with a capital "F," probably because I was totally stoned on pot at that time.

Me being a preacher just didn't seem to make much sense. I had never done well speaking to a group of people like that before. I thought, God, you must have the wrong number. Not me! No way am I preacher material. I am just a hillbilly that loves you Lord, so I would need to pass on that idea. Thanks but no thanks. But the Lord was tugging on my heart, and I shared this with Chaplain Dennis, and he was of absolutely no help when he started shouting "Praise God! Brother, the Lord wants to use you, fully use you man. You're called to serve Him." Later that night in the cell I got down on my knees by that hard steel jail cell bed, and I surrendered my heart and life to the ministry of the Gospel of Jesus Christ.

I thought that was one of the wildest things I had ever done. The next day I told Brother Dennis, and he said "Hallelujah brother!" be ready to share the Chapel Service Saturday night. The Lord allowed me to preach and start preaching right there in the Okaloosa County Jail. Yes, there are consequences to sin, but Praise God, there are also consequences to God's Grace. God redeems and restores broken and busted up lives.

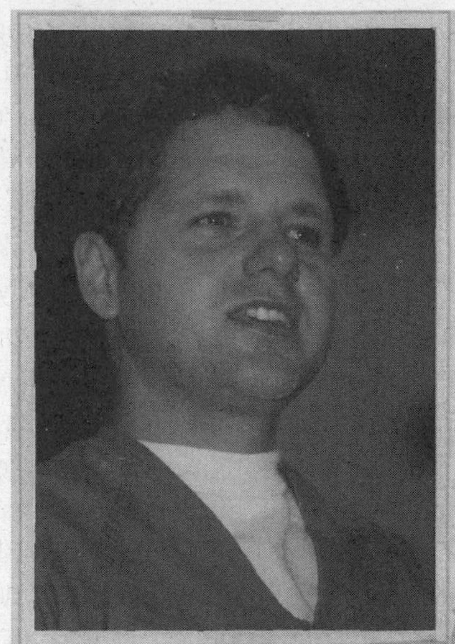

Preaching at County Jail

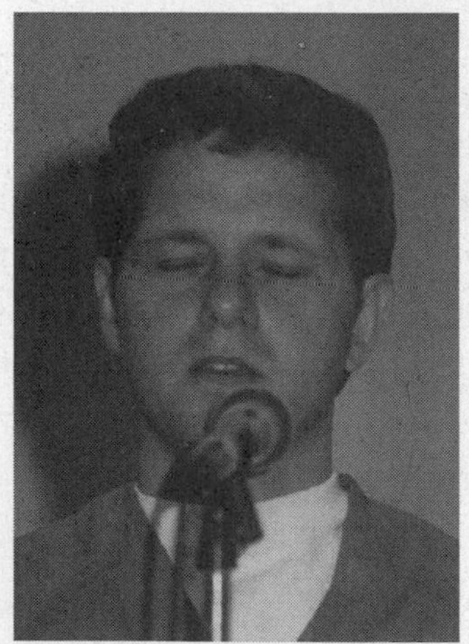

Mickey Closing Prayer County Jail Service

Chapter 19: Ninety Nine (99) Years Plea Deal

After sitting in the county jail for over a year, and all the legal wrangling and long Court hearing delays my court appointed attorney came up to the jail and shared with me that the State's Attorney had agreed to a plea deal for a Sentence of 99 years with the Court Retaining Jurisdiction over any possible parole release for 1/3 of that 99. I had been praying for God's will in all this, and even though that sounded awful, it could be a lot worse. It was better than a Florida Death Row Sentence, and to be honest, I was just tired of it all and just wanted to move on. The Lord had my back. I would trust in Him to lead, guide me and be with me.

In the County Jail as I was preaching, testifying and studying the Bible I had grown in my faith and my total trust in God. I had surrendered to the Lord, and I had promised that I would serve Him, if that meant going to Florida Death Row, or spending the rest of my life in Prison with a Life Sentence, I would be a Lifer for Christ. I would take Jesus to Death Row or wherever they sent me, to the deepest dungeons on earth.

I was on the JESUS TEAM and I was all in.

For me the chains were broken, the demonic bondage of the past was gone. I was like that demon-possessed man on the shores of Gadarenes when Jesus delivered him and sent the Legion of Demons into the herd of swine. I was now FREE from those shackles and chains of Hell. My heart's desire was to now tell others about this Glorious Savior who can and will set the captives free. It was no longer about what I did or had done but what He did and will do in a life fully surrendered to Him.

The Lord had blessed me in my time at the County Jail, I had started writing letters to a lot of ministries, pastors and youth sharing my testimony and many of these pastors wrote me back and shared how they had read my letter to the youth group or their Church congregation. How awesome and amazing it was that God was using me right there, right then from a jail cell.

I also was able to do a lot of Bible Studies and read a lot of Christian books. I got every Chaplain Ray Book I could get my hands on. This was a Prison Ministry out of Texas that published and mailed out books from Prisoners and shared their life-changing stories. I started doing all the Bible Studies that I could find and completed numerous Bible Certificate courses. I was even blessed to get enrolled into an external studies Bible College certificate program called Berean and completed the Youth Ministries credential study course. I had prayed in my jail cell for God to redeem the time in my life, and that I wanted so bad to finish my education and get a Bible College Education. The Lord was working mightily in all this and allowing me to redeem the time. Sometimes small baby steps are what it takes to get to the goal line or the top of the mountain of your dreams.

The light of Glory was evident in my life and I felt the joy and peace of the Lord even in the midst of a very bad situation. It was hard not knowing what the future would bring. It was a very hard and difficult time. I really didn't know what my future held, but I knew Who Held my future. The Lord Jesus Christ had my life, my future, my everything. He had the keys to my life. My trust was in Him and totally in Him.

On November 3, 1983, I stood in a courtroom and the Judge sentenced me to 99 Years to Prison with the Court Retaining 1/3 Jurisdiction over Parole Release for 2nd Degree Murder and Robbery charges. It was a heavy burden. It was a wheelbarrow full of time, as I was taken back to the holding cell I felt the reality of that burden as I pushed that wheelbarrow down the hall, and as I entered that cell, I felt something step in and a presence sort of just lifted that heavy weight and that overwhelming burden of that wheelbarrow. That something was someone and his name is JESUS! He will carry your burdens and come to you in your desperate hour of need.

After the sentence, while sitting in the holding cell waiting to be taken back to the jail, an officer came back to the cell and said they needed a picture for the court records. He had one of those Polaroid Instamatic Cameras. This was before digital cameras or cell phones, so he took a picture for the court records. I then asked him, "Officer Sir, could you please take one for my mother back in Tennessee." He said "sure" and I noticed the officer had tears in his eyes as he realized I stood there a condemned man to 99 Years in Prison. He took the picture and handed it to me and went back to the office.

I sat down on the bench there in the holding cell and watched as that picture developed in my hand. It took a few minutes to fully come into focus and as it did I looked at it and I saw a glow, there was this awesome radiant glow in my face and my eyes had a shine to them, the glow of Jesus and the light of Christ was shining in my face and the Lord spoke to my heart, "son, you are a changed man," *2 Cor. 5:17 Therefore if any man be in Christ, he is a new creature: old things are passed away; behold, all things are become new. I* ***was a new creature in Christ Jesus and the light of heaven was beaming in my soul.***

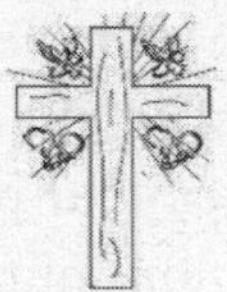

Chapter 20: The Road to Prison

Back at the Jail that weekend in the Chapel there was an amazing blessing. The Chaplain and his ministry elders came, and they held an ordination service for me. I was Ordained as a minister of the Gospel of Christ and as a Missionary to the inmates that I would encounter going into the Prisons. I would leave that jail as an Inmate Missionary.

Early the next morning the jail staff came and told me to pack my stuff, and they shackled and chained me and put me in the van for the ride over to the Butler Transient Unit the Florida State Prison Receiving and Diagnostic Unit in Lake Butler, Florida.

I had been on a lot of roads in life, from one end of the country to the other, from Mexico to Canada, from Germany to the Swiss Alps and now here I was on the road to prison. Where will the roads of life lead you? I never thought this would happen to me. I used to say like so many, "Oh that'll never happen to me!" But here I was shackled and chained on the road to Prison.

Driving up to the Prison it was still dark, and the razor wire, high fence, gun towers and bright lights were ominous as I looked out the window at the massive complex. They took me in and had me dump all my property so they could search it, then had me strip off my clothes, go through a shower to get sprayed for infestation, then get issued a set of Prison Blues. Next get the haircut, and then get your photo taken and a Florida Department of Corrections number issued. My unlucky number of the day was 091857, and then I was issued my bed linens and put in a line of other inmates and taken to the housing dorms.

While only there at Butler Transient Unit a short time, I was able to read my Bible and I started writing a Testimony Tract that I hoped one day would be printed and sent out to youth groups, schools, and juvenile detention centers. I titled it, "A Testimony of God's Grace to an Inmate."

After a few weeks, I got a notice from Department of Corrections Classification Office saying I had been classified to Union Correctional Institution, Raiford, Florida. I had no idea where that prison was, and I showed the paper to my buddy in the next bunk, and he turned white as Casper the ghost and looked at me in shock and said man that is bad news that is U.C.I. The Rock. One of the worst prisons in the State of Florida.

He shared that guards had recently been killed over there that it was a brutal place.

I thought Oh well, they must need a Hillbilly Preacher over there at the Rock. I'm just a missionary for the Lord. Wherever he sends me, I'll go. Wherever this road of prison leads me I will follow Jesus.

"NEVER ALONE: NO NEVER ALONE "

Looking out the window of the bus a multitude of rapid feelings flashed like lightning through my mind. It was all like a bad dream. What was I about to face? Would I make it? How would I make it through this? O' God I was so afraid, so alone. I literally trembled inside.

That was how it felt when the bus I was locked in rolled through the gates of the Maximum Security Prison in Raiford, Florida. Raiford was an infamous place. It was called "The Rock" as a nickname among inmates and guards alike, throughout the State Prison system it was one of the worst. Raiford's a hideous, ominous place of concrete, steel, high fence with razor wire and gun towers. It was an ugly place, but it had an even uglier reputation. Murders, homosexual rapes, violence, and hate permeated the place.

As I sat there looking out the window of the bus the feelings of despair consumed me. How could I handle such an evil, deplorable place? The gut feelings of fear sickened me. I had a gnawing fear and disgust at my life. These same feelings are experienced by thousands every year as there are some 2 million inmates incarcerated in the Prisons of America.

Each one of these wayward souls could tell of the despair, disgust and hopelessness one feels as they enter through the prison gates. The sense of total futility and feelings of loneliness experienced as one enters the world of prison cannot be described. Prisons are nothing more than society's garbage can. A Dempsey dumpster of sinful humanity.

I felt such an intense fear, dread, and loneliness. As a young Christian, I knew I needed God's help now more than ever. I'd gotten saved in the county jail 14 months before this eventful day, and I'd heard the chaplain say "Jesus is with YOU, No Matter What!" This was for sure a "No Matter What" moment for me. I'd heard and sang songs about the presence of Christ and that we're never alone, but would all that now practically apply to my fearful heart and hurting life?

I prayed a prayer for courage, for comfort and I asked God to please help me. Oh! If ever I needed it, I truly needed a touch of the Holy Spirit now. The words "Jesus is with you No Matter What" burned in my heart and soul. Would this day be a "No Matter What" day?

The Bible says in Is. 43:2 That "When thou passest through the waters, I will be with thee; and through the rivers, they shall not overflow thee: when thou walkest through the fire, thou shalt not be burned; neither shall the flames kindle upon thee." Daniel experienced a Holy presence and a cloud of protection in the Lion's Den. The three Hebrew children experienced His Holy presence in the fiery furnace.

These and many other examples of Scripture teach us that we are never alone, no never alone. I believe this is what Paul had experienced over and over again. He was able to say in some of life's most painful and fearful times, "My Grace is sufficient for thee: for my strength is made perfect in weakness. Most gladly therefore will I rather glory in my infirmities, that the power of Christ may rest upon me" 2 Cor. 12:9. Paul didn't preach a painless Christianity, but he knew that the power of Christ comes from the presence of Christ. That he was never alone, no never alone.

How does one experience individually the presence of Christ? Jesus said "For where two or three are gathered in my name, there I am in the midst of them. " Matt. 18:20. This might be a nice cliché for a Church picnic but does it apply in the dark, dismal moments of life? Does it really apply? What about the verse "I will never leave thee nor forsake thee" Heb. 13:5 Does it really apply? That searching questioned gnawed at my heart that morning as I stepped off the bus on to the grounds of one of the worst State Prisons in Florida, "The Rock."

I had prayed from the depths of my soul as we rode over the narrow county roads. I'd prayed silently but fervently in the Spirit as we walked in a small line to the processing room. I prayed continuously as we went from there to the laundry department to receive our issue of bed linen and prison blues uniforms. I prayed. Oh! Deep in my spirit and soul, I prayed.

As I stood there in line one of the inmate laundry workers walked by, and I heard him singing a melody to himself, "I've been redeemed, by the blood of the lamb." I shook myself as I was truly stunned. Was this really happening? A few minutes later the same man stuck his head out of an office window and said to all the new arrivals, "Hey! There's a great program over at the Chapel tonight at 7:30."

A heavenly joy filled me with praise as I realized here was a Christian brother. He was a light in the midst of darkness. I couldn't refrain myself any longer; I couldn't restrain my spirit anymore, so I said "Well Praise the Lord!" and looked at the man for his reaction. Sure enough, he lit up like a light bulb with a big grin and came over to me and asked, "Are you a Christian?" I answered, "Yes, a blood bought, spirit filled, full blooded one!" He said a louder "Praise God" and said hold on a second and left. I began to freak out, oh my God maybe he is a psycho and went to get a shank. Then he came back with another brother, a big huge fellow who looked like a giant to me, but he had the heart of a teddy bear. These two Christian brothers were like angels sent from God. They were used of God to minister to me in a time of desperate need. They would later help me get settled in and active in the Christian fellowship of the Prison community there. They ministered to me in my desperate time of need. The Lord will be with you "No Matter What!"

This was one experience that taught me the truth and reality of what it means that we are "Never Alone, No Never Alone." From the Rock to The Rock of Calvary, Christ Jesus is there.

No matter where you are, no matter what your circumstances are and no matter what road you're on, you are never alone, Jesus Christ is there.

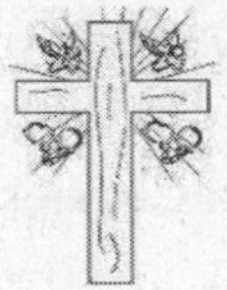

Chapter 21: "The ROCK Revival."

When I stepped into U.C.I. it was a very bad place and was full of evil, a lot of violence, deep darkness and hopelessness. But there was a large group of men who like myself had made a decision to live for Jesus where they were and were determined to be a strong beacon of Light in the darkness. That was totally awesome to me, and the Chapel programs were on fire for the Lord. Brothers were singing, playing guitars and worshiping the God of Glory full of Praise in that dark, dismal place.

The Light of Christ rose above the fog of evil and shined into the darkness of hell there. This place was a God given opportunity to grow in the Lord and to see the mighty hand of God move on hearts and lives of men. It was a place to see God move in my heart and bring spiritual maturity and direction in my life and my walk with Christ.

The Christian men who were at U.C.I. were more than just friends, homies, or chain-gang homeboys; they were brothers and family to me. These brothers were there for each other if I hurt they hurt, if one had family hurts or problems we all stood together in tears and prayers. It was a bond of brotherhood that has carried over even until today. Many of these men from that time are still friends and family to me.

There was a move of God and a revival there that was similar to the early Azusa Street revival in Los Angeles in 1901 and the revivals that had moved on people in the 1880's with Charles Finney and George Whitfield.

The move of God at U.C.I. was real and men who society had given up on and who were outcasts and castaways in life were finding deliverance, hope and joy in Jesus Christ. The Lord was working in so many men's lives, and the Chapel services were powerful, and the ministries and volunteers who came were filled full of the love and joy of Jesus Christ.

It was during this time that I began to seek the Lord for more of Him and His will for my life. I had asked the Lord to help me get a Bible College Education as that was a sincere desire of my heart. The opportunity came for me to be able to take some classes from a church-sponsored class in Minneapolis, Minnesota. One of the girls from that class started to write to me. Her name was Stacy, she and I became pen pals and began to encourage each other in the Lord.

Then I wrote to Luther Rice Bible College and Seminary in Jacksonville, Florida and shared my testimony and where I was and how I wanted so bad to continue my education and see God redeem the time in my life. This was the same school where many other great gospel ministers had went through. When I wrote that letter, I almost took the stamp from the envelope and threw the letter away thinking why send this and waste a good postage stamp. They will never give an inmate a scholarship. I was crazy to think so. But I mailed the letter and several days later I received a reply from Dr. Harwood Steele a Professor and Dean of Admissions at the school and he shared how they had gotten my letter and the faculty and staff were so touched by it. He shared that it would be an honor to accept me into their Bachelor of Arts in Biblical Studies program and that I would be the first inmate that they had ever granted this help to, and he prayed that I do well. He prayed that the Lord would bless my efforts and studies.

I was so overjoyed and full of excitement. I shared the news with one of my Bible study brothers Cedric Thomas and Cedric said oh how he wished he could get a Bible College education. That night I sat down and wrote another letter to Dr. Harwood Steele and shared with him about Cedric and how we were bible study brothers and he also truly had a desire to serve the Lord and would love to get a Bible College education. A few days later I got a letter from Dr. Steele saying, Dear Bro. Mickey it would be an honor to have Cedric enter our program of study with you. May God bless both of you in your endeavors and ministry.

One other awesome thing was Cedric was a black brother from Miami, Florida, I was a white brother from Chattanooga, Tennessee, yet we were family, we were brothers in Christ. That is Revival and the Real Jesus working in Real lives.

After two years and transferring credits from other classes and Bible certificate courses I was able to graduate with a full cap and gown graduation ceremony at the Chapel of U.C.I. with a Bachelor of Arts in Biblical Studies. Six months later Cedric graduated as well with a

Bachelor of Arts in Biblical Studies. Then after that and with the support and sponsorship of Harold Morris's prison ministry, we both were able to continue and get our Masters Degrees in Ministry from Luther Rice Seminary. God blesses us in so many ways as we just trust and follow him.

Psalms 37:3-5 Trust in the Lord, and do good; so shalt thou dwell in the land, and verily thou shalt be fed. Delight thyself also in the Lord and he shall give thee the desires of thine heart. That is a precious promise from the Word of God, and as I continued to write Stacy, I had another deep and special desire brewing deep in my old hillbilly heart.

Bunnie, Mickey and Cedric
@ The Rock

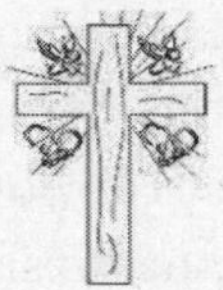

Chapter 22: Espoused By The Spirit "A Love Story from a Missionary's Prayer"

("For thou are great and doest wondrous things: Thou are God alone." Ps. 86:10).

That is a truth that flows from the depths of our souls as we see the majesty, glory, and sovereignty of God in our lives. As we look at His ways and His works we truly can sing unto him, sing psalms unto him: talk ye of all his wondrous works." Glory ye in His holy name; let the heart of them rejoice that seek the Lord" Ps. 105:2-3. Often times we are all prone to wonder if God really cares, or if He even truly hears our prayers. As a testimony of God's love and care for us, I want to share a short story of our Lord's marvelous providence.

Perhaps no other decision or concern of life is more important to a young woman or man as the pressing concern as to "Who will be my mate, helpmeet, and partner for life?" To a young Christian, this is a very important matter. So then intermingled with the choices and options of a career, there lies the deep desire for a husband or wife.

This was so true with Stacy, as a young missionary, who had surrendered to the call of God upon her life, she had a deep, intense desire to serve the King of Kings and the Lord of Lords, Jesus Christ in any and every way He chose. She had committed her life to the bone and marrow of her soul to go wherever He would have her go, to do whatever He would have to do. But still deep within her heart was that desire for a husband, that yearning for a co-laborer, a companion, and partner in Christ.

On a hillside overlooking Port-Au Prince, Haiti where Stacy was on her first real missionary assignment with Teen Missions she lifted up a prayer from the depths of her soul. She committed her young life first of all to God's service and asked Him to bless her desire for a helpmeet. Then and there in the summer of 1983, she laid that deep desire for a husband on the altar of prayer. "Father, I surrender to serve you, and wherever you lead me, I'll follow. Lord, you have a husband for me, and I commit this desire to you. I will serve you faithfully, with or without a husband, because Lord I know that you know best." Stacy could relate to that verse Jeremiah 33:3 "Call unto me and I will answer thee and show thee great and mighty things which thou knowest not." Stacy was about to taste the sweet and sometimes sour reality of this truth.

The summer being over and upon return to the States, Stacy began working and striving toward her goal to eventually be a medical missionary. Soon to enter nursing school and now back home in Minnesota, she was active in fellowship and ministry at her local church Fridley Assembly of God. Stacy began to seek open doors of ministry opportunity. When doing her devotions, she would come across scriptures such as Hebrew 13:3 “Remember those in bonds as bound with them which suffer adversity, as being yourself also in bonds.” James

1:27 "Pure religion and undefiled before the father is this. To visit the fatherless and widows in their affliction, and to keep himself unspotted from the world."

Stacy also prayed and felt the Lord whispering to her heart about the neglected and often forgotten elderly, widows, and prisoners. Both the scriptures and what the Lord was speaking to her heart about were very much upon her heart. It was during this time that in a Sunday evening service at Church a testimony was read by a Bible professor's wife. Ken and Allison Chant represented Vision College and had been active in helping an inmate in a Florida prison take Bible College courses through correspondence. It was a letter from Mickey Park from a Florida Correctional Institution thanking them for sponsoring him and enabling him to take the courses through Vision College and praising God for His wonderful Love, Mercy, Grace and Redemption.

Stacy felt compelled to go and ask Mrs. Chant for the address where she could write to Mickey. Mickey could have been a 65-year-old man it didn't matter; the Lord just let her know that she was to write Mickey and this was one of the reasons that the Lord had laid the Scriptures about prisoners upon her heart. Stacy had no idea what a marvelous plan God had in store for her life. She wrote to Mickey and just encouraged him in the Lord, letting him know she was praying for him and that Jesus was Lord of her life. She really didn't know if he'd even respond or not. Mickey received that letter in November of 1983 while still at the Butler Transient Unit of the Florida State Prison System.

Twenty-six years old and he had just received a 99 year prison sentence, unsure of tomorrow Mickey only knew a few things for certain, that in September of 1982 he had asked God to forgive him and for Jesus to be Lord of his life, that he was a free man now in Jesus Christ and had been called to minister and preach, to proclaim the message of Redemption and Reconciliation to the lost and hopeless. His year at Okaloosa County Jail in Crestview, Florida while awaiting sentencing had been a year of growth for him. Thanks to a committed Jail Chaplain, Brother Dennis, and his local prison ministry they had ordained Mickey as their first inmate missionary. This was a unique prototype ministry unheard of before. Chaplain Dennis and the Ministry wanted to send missionaries into the prison system. Mickey entered prison gates a missionary called and ordained by God and confirmed by the Spirit.

That letter from Stacy, being a young Christian sister was surely a lift and a great encouragement to Mickey as he sat on his prison bunk and read it. He was presently writing over eighty letters per month, most of these being ministry letters to youth. He wrote sharing his testimony and presenting the Gospel to them. What thrilled him most was here Stacy was a young person, not mixed up in sin or drugs or the world, but serving God. Stacy had touched this preacher's heart and soul and joyed him so.

For close to two years they would write and share a brother/sister in Christ love that flourished and glowed in a real pure and sincere way. They would cry and laugh as they would pray and share with each other over the phone whenever Mickey was able to use the phone. In the summer of 1984, Stacy would again go to the mission field, this time to Belize Central America. Mickey was at the "Rock" Union Correctional Institution, Raiford, Florida and would be fasting and praying for his sweet sister in Christ. He also committed to writing her as much as possible to encourage her and lift her up in the Lord. While all along Stacy continues to pray and trust God for that husband and helpmeet. She never thought or imagined that the hand of God was already working on this. She had a deep and special love in her heart for Mickey but yet only as a friend and brother in Christ. God had not yet unveiled His plan and will for her life.

Coming back to Minnesota and nursing school, Stacy continued to be active in ministry through her local church. The letters also continued to flow between her and the prisoner God had brought into her life. She sent him Scripture cards, little things that would lift him up. As he received letters from her at mail call, he would glow in the joy of the Holy Ghost, even so obvious that cell partners would notice and inquire what he was beaming about. More and more these two souls began to draw closer and closer. They shared a spiritual bond and union so special and rare as they shared their love for Christ with each other.

That love grew and grew until finally in the spring of 1985 God began to unveil His will and whisper to the two hearts knitted together in the love of Christ. Words can't quite adequately express the mystical depth of love that flowed between these two hearts and souls. Mickey began to hear that soft still voice of the Holy Spirit speak to him that Stacy would be his wife. He prayed over this and cautiously considered the seriousness, the risk, and the impossible odds involved. Being in prison and so uncertain of tomorrow was the greatest obstacle. He had never imagined or thought of ever falling in love while in prison with a 99-year prison sentence. It was the farthest thing from his mind. But he continued to feel this deeply spiritual and unique love grow for this woman who loved his Lord Jesus Christ so much. She was the real deal and boy he knew it. She was the love of his heart.

It finally came to the point where he had prayed so much and for so long and thought so much on this that he had to at least ask her. So he sat down at his desk, at his prison job where he worked as a Substance Abuse Facilitator and on that beautiful sunshiny day in May, Mickey wrote the most important letter of his life.

After all was explained and shared of his real and deep feelings and love for her and how the Lord was pressing upon his heart to share he closed with, “Stacy after you’ve prayed, and if it be the Lord’s will, would you “please, please, please, please, please, please, Please MARRY ME?” He wrote please seven times in memory of a course in Bible numerics, seven is heavenly perfection, and he felt he was seeking a marriage made in heaven. A physical union that had begun in a spiritual union.

After mailing that letter asking Stacy to marry him, the devil really attacked Mickey's thoughts. Telling him that he was a fool, "Boy you've really blown it now. Why there's no way she'll marry you!" He felt like he had done something so stupid and now probably lost a really good friend. Then word came from Stacy that she received the letter and that she just didn't know what to say, she would really have to pray and seek God's face on this. Add to this the fact that when Stacy had finished reading the letter, she left it on the table while she went out for a walk to think, pray and get some fresh air. When her mother came home from work, she noticed the letter from Mickey on the table and picked it up and read the letter. So now the news was out, and her mom knew. When Stacy came in the door, she saw her mother sitting there and immediately knew she had read the letter. Her mom asked, so what are you going to do?

Stacy just said I don't know mom, I am going to have to just pray over it. This placed an immense amount of pressure on Mickey. Here he sat in prison unsure, uncertain and not knowing what would happen and this was really hard emotionally.

Then one night, in the early morning darkness Mickey knelt down beside his prison bunk there in his prison cell and wept to God. He laid it all upon the altar of prayer and experienced the warm, sweet peace of Jesus permeate him, and the presence and fullness of the Holy Spirit filled him and refreshed him. Although it was only May and it would be some two months later in July when Stacy finally replied and said "YES!" she too felt it would be an honor and the will of God to be Mrs. Mickey Park. Truly words can't express or describe the joy and glorious praise that flooded Mickey and Stacy's hearts at this time.

Ironically they had never even met face to face, but had only seen pictures, talked on the phone, and shared letters through the mail, Stacy would play her guitar and sing Christian songs to Mickey, and they wrote hundreds of letters while the Lord cultivated a pure, holy, deep and intense love between and within them.

It was October of 1985 when they'd finally get to meet. In a knee shaking, inner trembling and butterfly episode they met in the very county jail where Mickey had received Jesus into his life and accepted his call to the ministry. As he was back at the county jail for a Court hearing. This only led to solidify and confirm it more, that they were a match made in heaven and truly intended for one another.

After that visit, Stacy went on a short mission's trip to Nigeria, West Africa. It was there that she felt the Lord speaking to her heart that her place was to be beside Mickey, to be a ministry to him and with him. Upon returning to Minnesota, she began packing her duffle bag and guitar case and making plans to move to Florida.

That was February of 1986, and on Valentine's Day, they began a season of togetherness that God has continued to nurture and bless abundantly. Espoused and promised to each other they walked in a joy and a peace that passes all understanding. In the fullness and freshness of the Holy Spirit, they walked on with the Lord Jesus Christ in the pilgrimage of life. Mickey was still in prison but they were content and assured that yes, God does care and yes God does answer prayers as they were Espoused By the Spirit.

Photo of volunteer Ruth (Mom) Barron, me, and Stacy
At the Okaloosa County Jail, October 1985
(Our first time meeting face to face).

Stacy and Mickey at the Rock Visiting Park
(Union Correctional Institution)

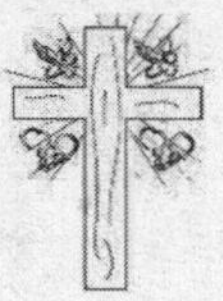

Chapter 23: The Prison Journey

Now with Stacy living close by and moving to Florida, it was really wonderful to be able to get regular visits on weekends and holidays. It was such a special feeling to have family and someone I loved and cherished to spend time with, to cry with, and to pray with.

I know that it was hard for her, as she had to stand in visiting park lines and go through visiting park shake downs. The guards could be sweet, or they could be sour, it was just a toss of the coin on most days. She would try and come early and beat the long lines and large crowds. She also began to become friends with several women who had men at the Prison at Union Correctional Institution. That gave her an opportunity to minister to them and be ministered to by them.

Stacy felt led to do a small startup women's ministry to help women who had to travel long distances to visit their inmate loved one. She rented an old dilapidated house in Lake Butler, Florida and was at least able to offer the women a bed, something to eat and a safe place to stay when they visited. We both prayed about what ministry the Lord wanted us to have, and she felt the Lord give her a name for our Ministry, it would be Set Free To Serve Ministries.

I really loved that name as it matched one of my favorite verses, **John 8:36** ***If the Son therefore shall make you free, ye shall be free indeed.*** So our ministry "Set Free To Serve" was started while I was in prison at the "Rock" at U.C.I. in 1986. God used us to minister and bless so many families and we made some very special wonderful friends who became like family for life.

Even with Stacy now living close by, life in prison was not easy. It did help to have her close, but it also added the stress of being concerned about her and how she was going to make it. One day in the visiting park the guards rushed in and sent all the visitors home. There had been a hostage situation in medical, and the prison was put on security lockdown. Another time we were sitting in the visiting park, and we saw one inmate beating another with a big stick out on the compound, we saw the security squad rush in and tackled him. She witnessed some of the hard and harsh reality of prison just by visiting.

Stacy got a job as a nurse, and was blessed to befriend some local prison ministry volunteers Don and Nita Weston, they became friends and family to her. Mr. Weston was a carpenter and painting vocational instructor at the prison and a Baptist minister who had a love for prisoners and their families. They were so full of love and were such an encouragement and help to Stacy and the other U.C.I. inmate wives and families.

I began to see how God was using prison ministry

volunteers to become part of our lives and be the family I never really had. It was so wonderful to see how the Lord used these volunteers in a time of my deepest need.

Some were Prison Fellowship volunteers some were just local church people, some were pastors, and some were Sunday school teachers. All of them full of the Love of JESUS and a Heart of Gold.

There was one special man, Johnny from Hattiesburg, Mississippi that had been corresponding with me and writing and sharing Bible studies and encouraging me in the Lord. Johnny drove all the way from Hattiesburg, Ms. to Raiford, Florida to visit me. Prison ministry people were my only real family. I never had visits from any of my family in Tennessee. My dad was a homeless alcoholic on the streets of Miami, my mom a chronic alcoholic up in Tennessee. So in a time where I needed family, God sent family, and that family for me was Prison Ministry Volunteers.

At the Rock, they even had a children's Sunday school program where a local church group of volunteers came in and with a few select inmate chapel helpers they would take the Children from the visiting park to the chapel and have a Children's Sunday school class. Stacy and I were approved by the Chaplain to participate in this and it was so great for us. We also met a wonderful Christian widow lady Mrs. Myrtice from that church who became like family to us.

Although I was very settled at U.C.I. I wanted to move closer to Chaplain Dennis and his ministry and felt a need to ask for a transfer to a Prison closer to them. The Lord would move me from U.C.I. to A.C.I. West Unit. The Apalachee Correctional Institution in Sneads, Florida was a much more relaxed camp with more work details with a large vocational program and a very good chapel program under Chaplain John Paulk. Chaplain Paulk had even completed a new chapel building campaign using the support and donations from the local churches and businesses. He was an old-fashioned Wesleyan preacher who preached a powerful and life changing challenge of the Gospel every Sunday morning.

The first Sunday after I had gotten to A.C.I., Stacy and I were in the visiting park when Chaplain Paulk came out and asked us to come to his office with him. As we sat down he said "Mickey I have some sad news, your Aunt Susie called this morning and said your sister Linda has died and your aunt would like you to call her." He let me call my Aunt Susie in Tennessee from his office phone. It was there I learned that my 37-year-old sister Linda, had become an alcoholic just like our mother and she died all of a sudden from a viral illness. I shared that day on the phone with Chaplain Paulk and Stacy sitting there that my life was changed, that I was a new creature in Christ and I was so sorry that Linda, my cousins including my aunt's daughter, Danette who was on drugs and my entire family didn't have this joy and freedom that I have even while in prison. That freedom being in Christ Jesus.

After the phone call, Chaplain Paulk was so touched that he prayed with Stacy and I. Later that week I asked him if he could use a Chaplain's clerk and he worked it out so I could work there at the prison Chapel as one of his Chaplain clerks. It was an amazing time to grow and see God change men and become real for Jesus. One of the chaplain clerks who became a dear friend, brother and family was Rob. Rob played the piano and sang like an angel. God had given him not only a talent but an anointing from on high. Rob and I ended up bunk partners in our dorm and we shared everything if I had a soup or Little Debbie cake he had one; if he had a soup or little Debbie Cake, I had one. We were family and praise and Glory to God still are. During this time Stacy had also moved to Sneads, Florida near the prison and she became friends with so many prison inmates family and the prions ministry volunteers.

The Florida Prison system was under a massive growth due to crack cocaine and all the drug offenses. They built several new prisons in the North Florida Panhandle, and out of the blue one day a bunch of us were told to pack it up and get ready to be moved to Holmes Correctional Institution in Bonifay, Florida. I had never heard of Bonifay, Florida and didn't want to move but there was nothing I could do. It was a brand new facility and I went to work for the Chaplain as his Chaplain clerk. The Chaplain had volunteers come in and preach one night a week, in addition to his Sunday service. These prison ministry volunteers were all preachers or teachers from area churches.

One of these Preachers was Brother Gary Gibbens. He came in and was very similar to Chaplain Paulk, he preached his heart and soul out and would plead with men to accept Christ and let God change them and turn their lives around. I began to just love that red headed brother and his preaching and how it challenged and encouraged me to be real and to stand up and fight the devil to see souls saved and lives changed. Gary and his wife Debbie became dear friends of ours. At times they would come in and visit with us at the visiting park.

They would bring with them their two young boys Daniel and Jeremy. I will never forget the joy it was to be able to wrestle and play with those boys out in the grass in the little fenced in Visiting Park at Holmes Correctional Institution. I, who had no family, yet how the God of glory had provided me a family. A family of prison ministry volunteers.

One morning there at Holmes C.I., the Chaplain called me out to his office early, he told me that my brother Mike had called and wanted me to know that my mother had died the night before and that he wanted me to call him. The chaplain let me call my brother Mike in Tennessee and he shared that my mother had lost her battle with alcoholism and had died of Cirrhosis of the Liver at Erlanger Hospital in Chattanooga. I was stunned but not surprised. I just was thankful that my mom had been able to visit me a short while before that, thanks to Stacy's mother getting my mom a bus ticket so she could visit me at A.C.I. She and Stacy had a few days to spend together and we all enjoyed the time to visit.

After the phone call, I went back to my dorm and picked up the Bible that she had given me that had been hers at one time and read ***Ps. 119:50 This is my comfort in my affliction: for thy word hath given me life.*** I highlighted that passage and wrote the date 6/13/89 H.O.C.I. (Mother's death) out to the side. Drugs and alcohol, Satan and sin had destroyed my life and continued to cause pain and heartache. Because of my prison sentence and time I never got to attend any of the funerals just the phone calls and then the heartbreaking messages.

After being at Holmes C.I. for about a year, I was

able to get my custody reduced from medium to minimum custody. That was a real blessing, and that meant I could do work details outside the prison gates off the compound. I put in a request to go to a work camp in Marianna Florida, Jackson Work camp was a very small facility that was in the city of Marianna and supported work details for the city and county. Getting moved there was a blessing because there was no fence or razor wire, and Stacy could bring in home cooked food.

I felt maybe this would be a step toward a parole consideration and a step toward getting the Court to see that I was a candidate for parole. The Judge still had the Jurisdiction over any parole consideration, so it was still a big obstacle. Even if the Parole Commission wanted to Parole me, the Judge would have to agree, and most of the time the Parole Commission would not even consider a person for release until the Court had released that jurisdiction. I was just so thankful to be at such a relaxed and minimum security place.

Visitors and families were able to bring home cooked food to the visitation, it was like a picnic outside in a small park. The place was so relaxed, peaceful and calm. There was a small puppy that was a stray that came up one day, and I asked the Major if I could keep it for the weekend and give it to my finance Stacy. He let me keep the dog and give it to her that weekend at visitation. We named the German shepherd puppy “Mugsy” as he broke out of prison.

The peace and calmness at the work camp was so refreshing, there was no high fence, no razor wire. It was like the Lord was showing me, that He was getting me ready to be released back into society. It was sort of a refreshment from the years of doing hard time in the hard core prison facilities. I could relax and breathe in the freshness of each new day as I studied my bible, prayed and dreamed of the future ministry that Stacy and I would be part of.

The chaplain over the facility even let me preach a service once a month. He was such a neat Christian man and encouraged me in so many ways. He was willing to share his pulpit with me, as he wanted to let me grow and learn in the ministry. God was blessing in so many ways. The dreams of ministry of evangelism were coming true.

Then tragedy struck. Some inmate at one of the minimum custody camps in another part of the State escaped and killed a person. So the Florida Department of Corrections ordered all violent offenders in the State back to close custody security status and back to maximum security facilities. The prison journey just got devastatingly painful and sickening again.

The Major at the work camp had tears in his eyes when he had to come and tell me that they had to ship me to A.C.I. West Unit. That was a dark day for me and for Stacy as well. It was devastating to us both. A day of shattered dreams and shattered hopes.

It was such a painful and hard time to have to go back to a major prison after such a sweet and refreshing time like this. It hurt, Oh! it hurt so much and so deep.

Mickey & Stacy @ A.C.I. Visiting Park

Mickey & Stacy @ A.C.I.

Mickey's Mother, Stacy & Mickey 1988 A.C.I. The only and last visit he would have with his mother. She died shortly after of alcoholism.

Mickey's Sister Linda's grave site. Died @ 37 years old.

Mickey & Stacy at Holmes CI

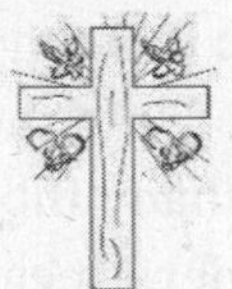

Chapter 24: The God of Glory, Comfort and Redemption

The trip back to A.C.I. was really a hard time for me. I had been gone for over two years to Holmes C.I. and then to Jackson Work Camp, and it seemed like things were looking good for a parole consideration with minimum custody and working outside in the community. But all that was gone in a matter of a few hours. I was so disappointed and hurt. Devastated.

Life is like that sometimes, though. I know that in life we face ups and downs, good times and bad times. For me, as a child of God, I have a trust that He is in control, not only of the good times but also of those dark bad times in life. This tragic life challenging event in my life just made me draw closer to Him and to go deeper. *Jeremiah 29:11 "For I know the thoughts I think toward you, saith the Lord, thoughts of peace, and not of evil, to give you an expected end."* I knew that God had a plan and purpose for my life and part of this experience and the pain and disappointment was all part of His plan to take me deeper in Him and His great Grace.

I was able to get back in with Chaplain Paulk, and that was a blessing for me, and I also decided that I had the time now to go ahead and complete some more Bible College. To let God use this time in my life to redeem the time. I was able to enroll into the Doctorate of Ministry Degree Program at Bethany Bible College in Dothan, Alabama. So what the devil meant for evil, God was going to bring good out of this ordeal and praise God he had already started.

I worked in the Chapel and worked on my studies, and I also worked on writing gospel tracts and pamphlets and had them printed with Stacy and other volunteers help. I was amazed at how God allowed me to reach outside of those prison fences with the message of Hope and Deliverance. Several major ministry organizations helped to print and distribute some of my tracts. The American Tract Society did one of mine, then Harold Reynolds Evangelistic Ministries printed and distributed hundreds of thousands of my tracts and pamphlets to Prisons and Jails. Including one I had written from Holmes C.I. a booklet titled "Stepping Stones To Prison." My testimony tract was also being read on some Christian Radio stations, and it was exciting to see God touching lives and using me from A.C.I.

CBN 700 CLUB does my Testimony

While at A.C.I. and doing the ministry outreach from behind prison fences, the CBN 700 club had a T.V. crew come down to the prison, and they did a testimony feature of me and the power of God's Grace to redeem and renew a broken life. That was totally amazing to think that not only were there hundreds of thousands of my testimony tracts being distributed by ministries, but now the CBN 700 club feature would touch millions of viewers.

I had asked God to redeem the time and make something good come out of the devastation of getting sent back to a maximum security Prison and Glory to God He was doing it in awesome and mighty ways beyond my wildest dreams.

Doctorate of Ministry Degree

The Lord allowed me to use this time to grow in trust to Him and also to bless me with my desire to redeem the time. The final classes were completed from Bethany Bible College, and I was allowed to have a full cap and gown graduation ceremony in the Chapel at Apalachee Correctional Institution with the Professor coming over to bestow my Doctorate of Ministry Degree upon me during a Sunday morning chapel program.

What an Awesome God we serve.

This was a dream come true, and I had worked so hard to see it actually happen.

Yes! Praise and Glory to God! He does redeem the time in our lives and takes back what the devil has stolen and destroyed. From a High School kick out, to a college dropout drug addict alcoholic to a Doctorate in Ministry Degree. That is the God we love and serve who can take one from Rock Bottom to the Rock of Calvary! That is the glorious power of Jesus Christ to redeem broken, busted up lives.

The Lord also used this time to bring comfort to me and to open doors that I would never have had open had I not came back to A.C.I. One day Chaplain Paulk was talking with me, and he told me that it would be good if I could get a vocational certification he felt that with my parole hearing considerations that it would help to have some job skills or vocational training. The prison had a program that taught inmates how to do CAD drafting, Computer Automated Drafting and Design was learning software to design engineering and architectural drawings and was a high demand job field. It was time to go for a change, and he said he would call the supervisor and see if he could put in a good word to get me into the program.

It was a difficult decision to leave what I loved and the comfort of working in the Chapel, but this was another one of those opportunities to redeem the time. So I took it as an open door from God to go through. I had never touched a computer much less ever planned to be working from one as a professional. Are you sure about this Lord? I was allowed in the program, and I worked hard and began to really enjoy the AutoCAD drawing and designing engineering and civil mapping drawings. Plus they paid like 65 to 70 cents an hour, so that put a little money in my account for Little Debbie Cakes, Ramen Noodle soups, Cheetos and fish steaks to make that famous Ramen Noodle chain gang Goulash and even helped me send money to Stacy to help cover our phone bill. It was a good program, and you did learn real-world work skills.

While back at A.C.I. Stacy and I continued to grow in our love and commitment to each other. I had been up for several parole hearings, and they had most often said "No Change" or reduced just little off my parole date. Stacy had been to those hearings over and over again, and we both would be so devastated and disappointed and hurt when they said No. It was one of these hearings that really knocked the emotional and spiritual breath out of me.

It was so hurtful, and even more hurtful to see my dear Stacy have to suffer and go through this pain for me and because of me. She deserved better, and at times I would pray and talk to God as I walked the rec track there at A.C.I. or as I sat on the bleachers by the ball field or weight piles. I would get alone and pray and ask God if we needed to just move on and let Stacy move on with a life without being tied to an inmate rotting in prison.

We had discussed getting married, but Stacy felt and believed God was going to give us a Church wedding. We had been engaged and walking this prison journey almost 10 going on 11 years now. Parole denial after Parole denial and it was not looking too promising.

What kind of life was that? I prayed and asked God to please help us and strengthen us to press on. The Lord spoke to my hurting heart and whispered, **"Just keep praising me, just keep praising me and press on!"** ***Isaiah 61:3 To appoint unto them that mourn in Zion, to give unto them beauty for ashes, the oil of joy for mourning, the garment of praise for the spirit of heaviness; that they might be called trees of righteousness, the planting of the Lord, that he might be glorified.***

That was certainly not easy, but it was possible, and I pressed on in praise and continued to trust the Lord to help us and comfort us in our Love and Relationship. It was shortly after this that I got this letter from an aunt in Tennessee whom I had never even met. It was my Aunt Kathryn and one of my dad's sisters. She had retired from her job and moved from Escondido, California back to Tennessee. She shared that she had gotten my address from my Aunt Betty in Oregon. She shared that Betty had told her about my getting in some trouble in Florida and the situation and that she wanted me to know that she loved me and wanted to come down and visit me.

That was one of those "WOW!" moments in life when you just sit and cry and say what a mighty and glorious God we serve.

Aunt Kathryn and her husband George came to Florida from Tennessee to visit Stacy and I. This was just an amazing and unbelievable blessing to me. Here was a sister of my dad's that I had never even met coming in the visiting park of a Florida Prison to visit me and encourage me. She shared how she had bought some property right outside of Chattanooga out by the Tennessee River in the hills. I knew exactly where she was talking about because I used to swim in the spring right next to her property. We had a rope swing, and we would all swing off into the water from these big boulders and rocks. She shared a lot about my dad and how they would have fun together, and all her other brothers and sisters. It was stories of my family, and yet a family I had never known. It was like God was answering more of those deep prayers to redeem the time in my broken life.

As it came time for visiting day to end and Stacy, Aunt Kathryn and George were getting ready to go; Aunt Kathryn asked what she could do to help me. I shared I really don't know other than I need to get a Christian Attorney to help me present my case to the Judge and Florida Parole Commission. We all hugged and said our goodbyes. She left the prison that afternoon and was in Ft. Walton Beach, Florida the next day hiring and obtaining an attorney to represent me and take my case before the Judge and help me with the Parole Hearings.

God still moves and still works miracles today, just as yesterday. This was a God thing for sure, and it was totally amazing to experience.

The Department of Corrections was still building new prisons all over North Florida to keep up with the pace of demand, and they decide to move the CAD training program to Liberty Correctional Institution, in Bristol, Florida. So they packed us all up and put us on the Bluebird Bus, the prison system's Greyhound with no conveniences and took us to Liberty C.I. It wasn't that far from Sneads, so it was not much more trouble for Stacy to still be able to visit, she had to leave earlier to get there and get in line to be one of the first visitors let in.

Unfortunately and disappointingly, the Chapel program at Liberty was one of the deadest I had ever experienced. That was so sad because these men needed more and more was not there. They needed light, and the light was not there in the Chaplain.

Back then, the Chaplain had a good state job, and that was all it was to him. It was not a ministry or a calling. It was a job and a headache to him more than anything. He did little to encourage the Christian men or to seek a revival there. Even sadder was the fact there were not really any strong prison ministry volunteers coming, and that was mostly because the Chaplain did not encourage them to come or even allow them to come.

What I have learned in all this is that a good Godly Chaplain is worth their weight in gold. They make a ton of difference in how the program runs and if it is dead or alive. If you have a good Chaplain, and he has good volunteers that prison is blessed and going to be a shining light in the darkness. If not then it is a dark and spiritually desolate land.

During this time the attorney was hard at work, and he was able to build an amazing packet to present to the Judge to request that the court would relinquish the Jurisdiction over my parole. The Judge was the same man that had sentenced me 16 years earlier, and he was very familiar with the crime and with my accomplishments while in prison. The Lord used that attorney to present my case to the Judge in a way that it was overwhelmingly evident that I was a changed man. The Judge granted the motion and relinquished the jurisdiction and more less quoted in his order that I was a changed man. ***2 Cor. 5:17 "Therefore if any man be in Christ, he is a new creature: old things are passed away; behold, all things are become new."***

Graduation Dr. Mickey Park,
Bcthany Theological Seminary @ ACI

Dr. Mickey Park, Graduation group photo
Stacy's Mom, Sister Jeri Lee, Stacy, Debbie & Gary Gibbens and their boys Daniel and Jeremy.

Chapter 25: Work Release and Wedding Bells

Shortly after the Judge dropped the jurisdiction, the attorney was able to get a Parole Hearing and get a recommendation that I be sent to a Community Work Release Center to get an employable job and help transition me back into society.

I was sent to the Tallahassee work release center first as a step while I was waiting on a job offer to work out with an Engineering firm in Marianna, Florida which would be close to Stacy. This was such a blessing and such a joy as I was now at a small place that was the final step for men who were getting out. I knew God was working and working in an amazing way. I didn't have a parole release date yet, but this was a big step to get that parole release date.

It was also a place where visitors could bring in food and Stacy was able to bring me home cooked meals and a Waffle House pecan waffle. That was so cool after being locked up for 16 plus years. It was so great to have this taste of freedom.

While at the work release center my job assignment was with a small work crew at a local County park in Tallahassee. I was assigned to Bainbridge Park on Lake Jackson to help with maintenance and grounds upkeep. I loved it. It was so sweet after being locked up and confined for going on 17 years, what a blessing to be able to move around in such a beautiful park, and help keep the trails clear and the place clean and neat. To me it was such a blessing from God as I was able to go in the woods or on the trails or boardwalks and pray in the mornings and talk to God out in nature all alone just me and the Lord. After being in and out of Jails and Prisons for close to 17 years, always surrounded by prisoners or guards it felt so good to just be alone and to be alone with the Lord.

The chapel program at Tallahassee work release was from a prison ministry volunteer Bro. David who would come in during the week and do a bible study and then on Sunday morning he would come and take the guys to his church in Tallahassee. It was also here that on some occasions David would have Scott and Cindy Heburn come in and share. Cindy would sing, and Scott would share his testimony and teach the Bible study. I was so blessed by what I saw and heard. It was evident that God was real in this dude's life and Cindy had such a sweet, sweet spirit and was so gifted and talented in her guitar music and singing. I told Scott then in 1997 that when I got out on Parole, I would love to go in some jails, juvenile detention centers and prisons with him.

After a few months in Tallahassee, I was offered a job with an Engineering firm in Marianna, Florida and allowed to transfer to the Marianna Work Release Center. The Lord continued to work in an awesome way in my life. I was able to get a professional job in a professional engineering firm. I got up every day and went to work, and would return each evening to the Work Release Center. I went to a church in Marianna and was able to get visits from my prison ministry family over from Holmes C.I. Gary and Debbie Gibbens.

Stacy had always said that God was going to give her a church wedding. Well after 12 years of a long engagement that time had come, we had come to the place where we felt the Lord was working it all out. So we were able to have that Church wedding at a little Church in Grand Ridge, Florida. Stacy's mom, dad, sister, and brother in law came, also one of her close friends from Minnesota came down. Stacy had friends from her work attend as well. But I had no immediate family to attend, but I had a family. I had prison ministry volunteer family from all over the State of Florida attend. I had ex-inmates like Ken Cooper who had been at the Rock with me and now in Prison Ministry in Jacksonville, Florida. My Best Man was Don, an ex-inmate brother who had been with me at A.C.I. and the minister who performed the service was Rev. Don Weston, that Prison Ministry volunteer from the days at The Rock U.C.I., Gary and Debbie Gibbens the prison ministry volunteers from Holmes C.I. and Coretta Tindal and her son James who had been friends since the U.C.I. days, her husband did time with me at U.C.I. and had passed away a few years prior but they were so happy for us they drove up from Bradenton to share in our special day. Overall, we had about 25 prison ministry volunteers show up as our guest and family for our special wedding day. It was an awesome and wonderful day of experiencing the great glory of our great God.

That day was a strong testimony of how God restores broken lives and blesses sometimes even our wildest dreams to come true. How God will bless us in and through our most difficult and hard times. That wedding day was a miracle to Stacy and I. We had sat in visiting parks and prayed and cried and wept tears over the years as we faced an uncertain future. Now here we were that day seeing the Glory and Grace of God in a real and mighty way. That God is able, abundantly able to do things that we never imagined possible in our lives if we will only allow Him to have our lives. **Eph. 3:20 Now unto him that is able to do exceeding abundantly above all that we ask or think, according to the power that worketh in us.**

Wedding Picture (Oct. 18, 1997)

Mickey & Stacy cutting their Wedding Cake

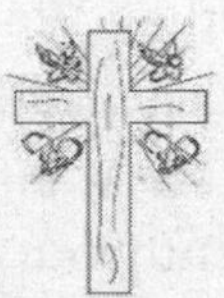

Chapter 26: Parole and FREEDOM

Not very long after the wedding the attorney was able to get the Parole hearing for my final release set. It still was not a done deal, and considering as much, and how bad I had been disappointed in the past I was not sure yet which way this thing might go. Stacy would have to go and be there, as they would not allow me to attend. It would be Stacy, the attorney and one of the engineers I was working for that would be there. I was stuck at work in Marianna praying and waiting on the phone call. It was a long morning for me. I was so nervous and wondering what was going to happen.

Then they called and let me know that I was going home the Parole Commission had voted "YES". I just burst into tears of deep, deep gratitude for a chance at Freedom again. This time it was real because almost 17 years ago I had found real freedom in a jail cell through the Lord Jesus Christ. I was so thankful and had a burning desire to get involved in prison ministry and juvenile jail ministry.

Shortly after coming home Stacy and I were able to go on a short weekend vacation to a Bed and Breakfast in Apalachicola. Florida and to St. George Island on the gulf coast to have a short honeymoon. It was totally so awesome and sweet to be able to go into the ocean and enjoy the beach together. We were so in love and now together. Totally unbelievable. The room had a small Jacuzzi bathtub, and she wanted me to have a bubble bath and relax. She accidently put too much bubble bath soap in, and that thing started overflowing with bubbles, bubbles and more bubbles until it started overflowing with bubbles. We had to bail soap suds down the sink to clean it up, but it was so funny and such a joy to laugh and giggle and be free. Free from the prison gates, razor wire and fences. We were free, covered in bubbles but free.

Getting to finally go home every afternoon to my new wife Stacy was such a tremendous blessing, and we were both so blessed. The little house we lived in was one she had gotten while I was at A.C.I. and it needed some minor repairs, so her mom and dad came down, and her dad helped me do some small projects like replacing the front porch and frame in a door on the garage shop. It was such an honor to have her dad show me the basics and help me learn skills I had never had the opportunity to learn. He gave me confidence on how to run a saw, swing a hammer and work with power tools and equipment that I had never used before.

Shortly after I got out and was working at the Engineering firm, I had to go for some software training in Miami. Stacy was able to go with me and we were able to stay at a very nice hotel on Miami Beach and walk the beach and enjoy the breeze together. It was so refreshing and nice to walk the beach holding hands, the prison fence and razor wire all behind us now.

While in Miami I wanted to try and find information about my dad. I knew he had been homeless there but had not heard anything from him in years. I had several chaplains from the Miami Rescue Mission checking and no one had seen him in a while as well. While on lunch break from the training class, I felt led to call the Miami-Dade County Medical Examiner's office otherwise known as the morgue to see if they by chance had any information. I called and told the man who I was, and I was trying to find out information on my father who had been homeless in Miami. I gave him the name Mack Mickle Park and his birthday Aug. 3, 1932, and I could hear him typing it into the computer. Then he came back on the phone and said yes sir, we had a Mack Mickle Park come through here in July 1995. I started to tear up as he said the cause of death was chronic alcoholism and a ruptured ulcer.

I then asked what they did with the body I thought maybe Stacy and I could take some flowers to the grave, and he explained that after 90 days if no one claimed the body they cremate the body and spread the ashes over the ocean. I said thank you, hung up and cried softly as I realized my dad had died a homeless alcoholic on the streets of Miami. I walked away from that phone with more reason than ever to step up my fight against the demons of hell and addictions. To take the Love of Christ and life-changing message of the Gospel of Jesus Christ to the lost and hurting homeless, to the drug addicted and alcoholic, to the jails, prisons, and streets wherever God would open the door I would go through it. Reaching those that I could with the Glorious Gospel of the Lord Jesus Christ.

Getting back home I was able to do some ministry with Scott and Cindy Heburn, and I also started volunteering with Teen Challenge Ministries in Graceville, Florida.

The prisons would not approve me to go in because I was on parole and had not been out long enough. Scott and I would minister at Dozier Boy's School in Marianna, Florida, a Children's home in Tallahassee, a Juvenile boy's center in Tallahassee and the Tallahassee Rescue Mission.

God was blessing me in so many wonderful ways in our home life and our jobs. I was blessed with another job offer for better pay and advancement with a large engineer firm in Tallahassee, and that was a big blessing.

Shortly after that blessing came another blessing and joyous surprise that we were going to have a baby girl. Stacy was pregnant and we were so excited that we were going to enjoy a little bundle of joy in our life. Our daughter Bethany Joy was born and we were so thankful and honored. So blessed. To me, it was a testimony of how Good and Great God really is and how He redeems the broken lives and restores the years the locust have eaten.

The Lord was blessing us in such a tremendous way. I was involved with Prison Fellowship and they did a feature article on me in their prisoner paper Inside Journal. It was a cool story about the redeeming Grace of God and had a picture of me holding my baby daughter

Bethany. That article was printed and sent into prisons all over America and touched millions of readers. Later I learned that snippets of that testimony article are still used today 17 years later in a Bible study course offered by Prison Fellowship.

I remember how in the county jail I had asked God to use me and let me shine the Light of Christ into the darkness of prisons, jails and drug recovery centers. I see now how God has been doing just that and using me to shine the Love and Light of Christ into the darkness of this world ever since the county jail.

INSIDE JOURNAL®
THE HOMETOWN NEWSPAPER OF AMERICA'S PRISONERS
VOL. 11, NO. 4, SPECIAL PRE-RELEASE EDITION 2000
PUBLISHED BIMONTHLY

Remembering His Chains

Ex-prisoner Mickey Park Makes the Leap After Hard Time

Seventeen years of prison time can institutionalize a man. But Mickey Park fought back. He replaced drinking and drifting while doing hard time at the "Rock" with Someone who transformed His life from the inside out—and then he met the other love of his life.

On a crisp, spring morning Mickey Park can hardly believe he's driving himself to work. At 43, the senior Computer-assisted Design (CAD) engineer finds life on strict parole "sweet as honey." But it was during his 17-year prison journey that the foundation for success was laid over a past of addiction and crime.

Mickey followed his father's lead early, picking up booze at age 12. "When [I] started drinking it was nothing to worry about, just a couple of teenage buddies drinking beer. No big deal," he says in his soft-spoken manner. He combined hard-rock music and pot and pills to round out his party life. By age 18 he married and joined the army.

He completed his GED, but chose the party lifestyle once again. He was told not to re-enlist, and his marriage ended in divorce.

Returning to his hometown Chattanooga, Tennessee, Mickey tried college on the GI bill. It lasted two years before the alcohol took over again. After a hit-and-run accident, Mickey saw no reason to keep trying the respectable life. Fearing the law, he left Tennessee and began drifting wherever the wind took him.

Eventually he hitchhiked his way to Destin, Florida. On the beach he met a young man at the warm water's edge. After sharing stolen beer and stories, the man suggested robbing someone he knew. Well into his third week of a continuous drunken fog, Mickey went along. The two hit the apartment, where Mickey knocked out the victim. He was helping himself to more beer when his new friend flew by him with a knife. Then "I realized this wasn't a simple robbery," Mickey remembers. Over the blare of

Continued on page 4

Prison Fellowship Inside Journal Article.

Remembering. . . *continued from page 1*

MTV in the next room, he heard hideous laughing. Walking in he found the victim dead.

The next day police caught Mickey driving the stolen car of the victim.

Hangman's salvation

In 1982 Mickey, then 25, awaited a murder trial in solitary. He reviewed the choices he'd made in life and concluded suicide would do everyone a big favor. "I was so bitter I flushed Gospel tracts in my cell down the toilet," he explains. "I thought, *Rather than rot in prison, I'll check out.*" He tied a sheet into a noose, placed his head in it, and hesitated. Remembering his devoutly Christian grandma, he decided to say a prayer to respect her memory. He got down on the concrete floor and asked "the Lord to forgive me and let me die."

Suddenly he broke into uncontrollable sobbing. Surprising even himself, he began repenting for his crime and of all his life's rebellion. In the midst of killing himself, he instead realized Christ had a claim on his life. Knowing almost nothing about Jesus, he nonetheless trusted his life to Him.

The next morning he requested a Bible. No matter what happened now, he knew he was God's property. His constant prayer was for God to make Himself real. In the meantime the state switched from seeking the death penalty to successfully winning convictions on both men and giving them life sentences—for Mickey, it was 99 years.

Next stop: Union Correctional Institute at Raiford, otherwise known as the "Rock." Possibly the worst cesspool in Florida, the Rock (now closed) was known for its horrific prison conditions and violence. A massive plant of 9,000 men, it reeked of its 40 years of oppression. But even here, Mickey immediately met other Christian inmates and got involved in the vibrant chaplain program. He also began writing letters, something that would prepare the way for his future.

Holding his infant, Mickey Park observes, "There are consequences to sin even after prison, but these are consequences to grace — I'm fully forgiven."

A love that waited

Mickey had begun correspondence courses and wrote a thank-you letter to a church that had supported him through the program. The pastor happened to read it aloud to his congregation so they could hear of his gratitude. Among them was a young woman, Linda*, who had recently felt led to somehow help the imprisoned and the widows. She wrote Mickey a letter of encouragement.

That began an unusual pen-pal experience. "When I got his first letter, it was obvious the Lord was in his life," Linda remembers. "He was a good friend for two years."

Both Mickey and Linda corresponded on purely friendship terms without anticipating anything more. He prayed, fasted, and even financially supported her with the little he earned as she went on mission trips to Haiti, Belize, and Nigeria. But then Mickey felt something more. But after some thought he hastily wrote a marriage proposal. "After mailing it I felt I lost a friend," he explains. "I've got 99 years. All logic goes against it. I felt bad."

It caused confusion for Linda, too. She knew the facts. She had to admit she felt something, too. But was this right? She took three months of prayer before answering "yes" to his letter in July 1986 with one condition—they wait until he was free. Linda required that condition out of respect to her parents' advice that she wait.

After a final overseas mission trip, she packed her bags and moved from Minnesota to Raiford to be near her fiancé. "My mother was a tremendous support praying for us," Linda explains about the unusual decision. "I never would have moved down to be with Mickey if she didn't have peace about it. It was hard for her to have a daughter in love with a man in prison."

Meanwhile, an exuberant Mickey began a series of legal attempts to gain early release. He had been a model inmate from the start, pursuing education and religious programs—but nothing worked. Every door closed.

So they waited. Years passed, and Linda kept busy with her job and made the best of her visits. Mickey pursued education, completing CAD training, and biblical studies through a Florida seminary.

During this time pastor friend and Prison Fellowship volunteer Don Weston provided accountability and guidance as Linda and Mickey struggled through a normally ill-advised relationship. "I'd been in the system awhile and knew lots of inmates with jailhouse religion," Don comments. "Many don't get inner healing and fall back into the same mistakes. I've seen many marriages pickle out—marrying and divorcing—before their release. So I was cautious [with Mickey] and watched."

Life after prison

In October 1997, after years of denials, a policy shift appeared. Lifers' records were getting consideration, and Mickey soon sat down to a sirloin steak and pecan waffle—his first outside meal in 17 years. For many, the idea of life outside after that kind of time is terrifying. Prison does little to naturally change inmates or their outside circumstances. But Mickey refused to take the numbing effects of prison lying down. What were the ingredients to his transition?

It started with a lifestyle of discipline—not routine. Routines aim to maintain the way things are. Discipline seeks to change them. Mickey wrote thousands of letters seeking help. He pursued every educational opportunity he could. He took advantage of strong chaplain programs. He worked prison jobs and completed new training. He waited rather than indulge in some of the legal and illegal pleasures of prison life. He kept the faith.

The DOC also granted him work release, which he [illegible]. He and Linda married after 14 years of waiting. With Linda and Don's help, he secured a job at an engineering firm using his CAD training.

Despite Mickey's 17 years of prison hardship, Linda can see the positive changes in him. With tears in her eyes she notes the benefits of having waited for God's best: "Many people with prison backgrounds can only think of themselves," she explains. "God really changed Mickey. He wasn't going to [illegible]. We do things by teamwork. We discuss and agree together. He loves the Lord, and me. He accepts me as I am and wants me to be all that I can be as a Christian woman—like going to college and furthering my education."

Mickey doesn't hear the screams of men in their cells anymore, but he does awake in the night to tend to his newborn baby. He doesn't worry anymore about his physical safety, but occasionally frets about bills and a problem car—a trade-off he'll take any day. Holding his infant and looking at his wife, Mickey observes, "There are consequences to sin even after prison, but there are consequences to grace—I'm fully forgiven." [illegible]

* Not her real name

Inside Journal Article continued (Mickey holding Bethany 6 months old)

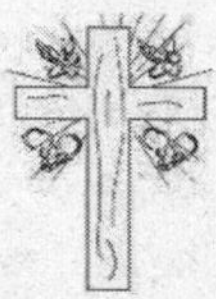

Chapter 27: Redeemed, Set Free and Delivered from Addiction

I have always been totally amazed at the story in Mark 5:1-20 of the demonic of Gadarenes, where Jesus comes to the shore and there he encounters a demon possessed man who had a legion of demons. The man was shackled and chained to a controlling demonic force and was an outcast of society. No man could tame him or control him. There was nothing and no one that could help that poor desperate soul. He was miserably hopeless. Controlled by Satan and his demons to the point of no hope for real deliverance.

Jesus stood there on the sea shore of Galilee and met that man in his hour of greatest need and commanded the demons to come out of him and they did and the people were amazed that saw the transformation and deliverance of that demon possessed man.

There he sit in his right mind and clothed, and the people could not believe it. It was a miracle behind comprehension. The power of God had truly redeemed, set free and delivered this man.

That same Jesus is still working today and is still able to redeem, set free and deliver those entrapped by the Satanic bondages of hell in drug addiction and alcoholism. He is able to break the shackles and chains of hell on a person's life that is trapped and tormented in the stronghold of addiction.

I have experienced the torment and pain of addiction personally and have watched it not only devastate and destroy my life but the lives of my family and friends. Addiction is a cruel taskmaster and will consume one's life like a cancer. It not only kills and sends one to an early grave but it also destroys and decimates lives to the very core of their being. Addiction will leave one's life busted and broken, totally destroyed.

Oftentimes people try to deny it, or they think they can fix it, and sort of like trying to fix a broken life with duct tape and superglue will try in vain to fix their addiction, their pain, and their problems in life. Those efforts will usually always be futile and only leads to heartache and failure. The inner pain and deep hurts and emotional damage that opens the door to demonic addiction is so life controlling and consuming you cannot just put a band-aid on it and call it good.

There is an inner pain and hurting heart that even the best Cardiologist in the world cannot fix. There is no surgery or any pill that will heal and fix the inner pain of the soul and heart. Like so, so many I have tried in vain in my life of addiction to kill that pain with drugs and alcohol. I have watched so many lives just evaporate into a dismal desperate despair of self-destruction as they try to kill that pain, that pain of living with drugs and alcohol addiction. I watched my mom, my dad, my uncles, my cousins and many friends all go to early graves through their addiction.

Graveyards are packed and prisons are full because of the demonic power and bondage of addiction. Today there are new and even more powerful drugs, synthetic concoctions from the very pits of hell that are more potent and more controlling than ever before.

There is also a prescription drug abuse epidemic that is just as deadly as heroin or meth. From the local pharmacy to the streets people are destroying their lives and futures and the lives and futures of their family and children with addiction. It is heartbreaking to see and to realize that it is destroying so, so many lives, so many homes, so many families.

I know what it is like to come from a broken home, and to come from a family broken and busted up by addiction. My uncles, my cousins, my mother, my father all died early deaths due to addiction. My dad died a homeless alcoholic on the streets of Miami, Florida.

The sad truth is that it usually creates a cycle of addiction and that child in that addiction environment becomes just like you. It becomes as I have shared a "Family Tradition." It becomes a cycle of addiction handed down over and over and over again.

The demonic power of addiction can be broken, just like that demon possessed man that Jesus delivered from those legion of demons, no matter how strong or how deeply embedded on one's life the demons of addiction can be broken by the Lord Jesus Christ. I can testify of that fact, I can testify of that truth. Hi, my name is Mickey and I am a Redeemed child of God, bought and paid for by the precious blood of Jesus Christ. I am redeemed through the power of the blood of Jesus, just like that old song, there is "Power, power wonder working power in the blood of Jesus Christ." It is more than a sermon and a song, it is real and JESUS changes real lives.

Glory to God, when all else failed, when the doctors and the programs and the jails and detox centers and all of man's efforts could not help me, the Lord Jesus Christ and His precious Blood Redeemed me. When I stepped out of prison at 41 years old, I had spent over 21 years of my life in and out of detox centers, programs, jails and prison. My friend that is what the bondage to addiction will do to one's life. But Glory to God I have been free over 20 years out of Prison, and I have been free in Christ Jesus over 35 years. Drug and alcohol free, free from the demonic subjugation of addiction. Free and full of the joy of Christ Jesus and able to enjoy a life full of His Love, Mercy and Grace. Free and full of the Glory of God's Grace.

You can be Redeemed, Set Free and Delivered from Addiction! Through the Lord Jesus Christ. He is the anchor of our souls, and His anchor holds when all else fails. No matter how bad the storm, or how high the waves of your life, or how battered your ship of life is, in Christ the anchor holds.

Chapter 28: Life Without

One evening I was sitting in the chow hall at Hays State Prison in Trion, Georgia ministering to a small group of inmates. Hays State Prison is one of the toughest and harshest Prisons in the State of Georgia Prison system. In 2013 there was a riot there and around the same time, it also experienced a Correctional Officer death and several inmates being killed by other inmates. The facility became one where the movement inside the prison was fully controlled and the Chapel services were only by a call out list by one dorm per week. All movement at the facility was strictly controlled. There was no longer a Chapel, and the chow hall was being used after the evening meal to hold Bible studies and Chapel Services.

Hays had become a hard core prison, and it housed some of the prisoners with harsh sentences and many of the men were serving life sentences. The way the chapel system was you never knew who would be at the Bible studies. That day the Bible Study group only had three men, and two of them shared that they had sentences of "Life Without." What that meant was that these two young men sitting in this small group bible study with me had Life without Parole sentences. A Life Sentence without the possibility of Parole consideration. A hopeless situation for sure and here we were. They needed Hope.

My teaching message for that day was ***"Hope: The Anchor of the Soul'***. I had not planned it that way, and I had not expected to be sitting there with a couple of men who were perhaps the epitome of hopelessness. But the Lord I love and share is the epitome of HOPE, and He is the Anchor of the Soul. I shared the message how we are to "Hope in God: Not in Man, Not in Circumstances!" Lamentations 3:22-24 **"Through the Lord's mercies we are not consumed, because His compassions fail not. They are new every morning; Great is your Faithfulness, The Lord is my portions, says my soul, Therefore I will HOPE IN HIM!"**

I shared how I knew this Hope was real, as it was real to me in my own desperate time of hopelessness. **Romans 5:1-5 "Therefore being justified by faith, we have peace with God through our Lord Jesus Christ: By whom also we have access by faith into this grace wherein we stand, and rejoice in Hope of the glory of God. And not only so, but we glory in tribulations also: knowing that tribulation worketh patience, and patience, experience; and experience, hope. And hope maketh not ashamed; because the love of God is shed abroad in our hearts by the Holy Ghost which is given to us."** The men's faces began to shine and glow, and they had a light in their eyes that was the shining light of the Hope of Christ.

I shared how **Hope takes Faith**:

I Thessalonians 5:8-9 "But let us, who are of the day, be sober, putting on the breastplate of faith and love and for an helmet, the hope of salvation. For God hath not appointed us to wrath, but to obtain salvation by our Lord Jesus Christ." How in his book "Disappointment with God" Philip Yancey shares "Faith means believing in advance what will only make sense in reverse." I told them about a little wall plaque that I have at home that has a powerful message on it that reads *"Let Your Faith Be Bigger Than Your Fear!"*

Hope Takes Help from God:

Hebrews 13:5-6 "**Let your conversation be without covetousness: and be content with such things as ye have: for he hath said, I will never leave thee, nor forsake thee. So that we may boldly say, The Lord is my helper, and I will not fear what man shall do unto me.**" Ps. 55:22 "**Cast thy burden upon the Lord, and he shall sustain thee: he shall never suffer the righteous to be moved.**"

Hope Takes Trusting in the Word of God:

I shared how I knew this Hope was real, as it was real to me in my own desperate time of hopelessness and that how through the Word of God the Lord spoke encouragement and hope to my heart.

Psalm 119:114 **"Thou are my hiding place and my shield: I hope in thy word."**

Hope Takes Power From The Holy Spirit:

Romans 15:13 **"Now the God of hope fill you with all joy and peace in believing, that ye may abound in hope, through the power of the Holy Ghost." Psalm 33:18-22 "Behold, the eye of the Lord is upon them that fear him, upon them that hope in his mercy; To deliver their soul from death, and to keep them alive in famine. Our soul waiteth for the Lord: he is our help and our shield. For our heart shall rejoice in him, because we have trusted in his holy name. Let thy mercy, O' Lord, be upon us, according as we hope in thee."** No man can give you this hope, the Judge can't give it, the Parole Man can't give it to you, your family or your homeboys can't give you the hope that only God can give us in our desperate hour of need.

Hope Takes Endurance:

Isaiah 40:31 **"But they that wait upon the Lord shall renew their strength; they shall mount up with wings as eagles; they shall run, and not be weary; and they shall walk, and not faint."** As Philip Yancey shares in his book that "Endurance is not just the ability to bear a hard thing, but to turn it into glory." God can and will bring Glory even out of this Prison time and out of our lives. In prison or out of prison we can experience His Hope, His Glory, His Love, His Mercy, His Grace. He breathes hope into the hopeless soul.

Hope Takes Patience:

Hebrews 6:15-19 And so, after he had patiently endured, he obtained the promise. For men verily swear by the greater: and an oath for confirmation is to them an end of all strife. Wherein God, willing more abundantly to shew unto the heirs of promise the immutability of his counsel, confirmed it by an oath. That by two immutable things, in which it was impossible for God to lie, we might have a strong consolation, who have fled for refuge to lay hold upon the Hope set before us. **Which hope we have as an anchor of the soul."**

The Cross of Calvary Beams Hope to the Soul!

Hope Is Possible Even When It Seems Hopeless:

Luke 18:27 "**And he said, The things which are impossible with men are possible with God."**

All I knew as I sat there with these men in that Georgia State Prison with sentences of Life Without Parole was that our God was able, abundantly able to give them the Hope they so desperately needed. That God was able to give them the peace that they so desperately needed. Even when all seems so hopeless, there is Hope, a hope not found in dope, or in money or in man's effort or man's solutions but a Hope found in Christ. This Hope is found at the Cross of Calvary through the blood of the Lord Jesus Christ. In Him and only in Him is there Salvation, Deliverance and True Hope. The Judge can sentence you to life, but only JESUS can give us abundant LIFE.

That day as I drove the 60 miles from Trion, Georgia back home to New Hope, Tennessee, I cried all the way home. I wept tears down my face for those brothers at Hays State Prison as I prayed and wept to God to Bless them and shine the Life and Light of Christ into the darkness of their lives. That even with Life Without, they could experience the fullness of Life Within, that Life in Christ JESUS. There is New Hope in CHRIST JESUS.

Chapter 29: The Tennessee Hills and His Glory

There was a time in my life when I just knew I would never see the beautiful Tennessee Hills or the rivers and streams again, or ever eat a home cooked meal or enjoy a mountain sunset. My life was at Rock Bottom, and that rock bottom was hard and harsh.

I had read a lot of books in prison. Some of my favorites were from Corrie Ten Boom. She was a lady from Holland and her entire family during World War II were sent to a German concentration camp for helping rescue Jewish people from the atrocities of the Nazis and they were arrested and sent to German death camps. In my Bible from prison, I had written a quote from one of her stories: ***"There is no pit so deep, that He is not deeper."***

God can reach into the deepest dungeon and redeem a broken, busted up life. That was a reality as I was packing up and we were getting ready to move back home to Tennessee. Stacy and I had been up to visit my

Aunt Kathryn several times, and we had talked about one day moving up there. When I was in prison Aunt Kathryn would dream of one day giving us some property so we could build on it and be close to her. One time while Stacy was visiting she walked up the side of the mountain behind my aunt's house and picked out a spot for us to one day build our house. Even before I had a parole date my aunt and Stacy were determined and believed it would happen. How amazing is that?

It was one of those life experiences where you just have to trust God. I had been working for an Engineering firm in Tallahassee and in 2002 when the economy began to slow down a lot of companies were laying off and I was laid off from my job. It was a time of uncertainty and fear even for the average most qualified guy, but I had a few things in my past that always could be a challenge to employment. I had learned that I just had to trust God to work it all out.

I had put in applications all over the area, and one evening I was out in the back yard and Stacy came out and said she had found a job ad online for a GIS Manager at a University in Tennessee. I thought you've got to be dreaming baby, if you think I have any chance at that. Well she submitted my resume and application anyway.

The next day I was home with Bethany being the stay at home dad while Stacy was at work and the phone rang. Well, it was the Professor of the Geoscience Department of Austin Peay State University, and he wanted to do a short phone interview. The only problem was that Bethany was in the middle of watching Barney the purple dinosaur and was jumping up and down on the bed singing "Barney, Barney we love you!" I was trying to turn the t.v. off and calm my little 3 year old down. I almost died of embarrassment and apologized to the professor, he just laughed and said O' no problem I have children also, I fully understand.

After the phone interview and later when Stacy got home, I told her about the phone call ordeal and how Bethany was jumping on the bed and singing, and I said to her there is "no way" those folks will ever call me back. Yet the next day I got a call again and was invited to come to Tennessee for a job interview, and despite telling of my past I was offered the job as GIS Manager. God has a future for us, we don't have to let our past define who we are today.

Now here we were moving up to Tennessee to see a dream come true. I had been offered a new job with Austin Peay State University in Clarksville, Tennessee as the GIS Manager. It was a tremendous opportunity for me professionally and for my career. Stacy and I went to Clarksville for the job interview in December 2002, and we just loved the area. It was a chance to get us to Tennessee and eventually we would get closer to Aunt Kathryn.

Moving to Tennessee was such a blessing to me, as it brought me back to the mountains and hills I loved and cherished. I am so thankful and so amazed at how the Lord has redeemed and blessed my life. Stacy and I both had good jobs; we had a deep love for each other and Bethany. We had seen dreams come true. Every day we were walking miracles in the Love, Mercy and Grace of God.

It is amazing how the Lord works sometimes. It just blows my hillbilly mind away. A short while before moving to Tennessee I had applied to move to Minnesota, and the State of Minnesota rejected the interstate parole compact request. That closed one door, and then this door with this awesome job in my home State of Tennessee opened. Only God could have worked that out the way it did. It is totally amazing how the Lord works in and through our lives. There is another quote in my Bible from one of Corrie's books that says: "When one door closes another door opens. We often look so longingly after the closed door that we fail to see the one which swings open to us." The Lord has a plan and a purpose for our lives, we just need to trust Him and follow Him.

While we were in Clarksville it was also time for a Parole release hearing, and we needed to drive down to Tallahassee, Florida to attend that hearing. The Tennessee Parole officer wrote a very strong letter of recommendation and felt sure that they would drop the parole supervision. I had been out on parole for over 5 years and been doing great. I had a professional career, had a stable home environment, involved in Church. I was doing everything and more to exceed what they wanted me to do. There was nothing else I could do.

The Tennessee Parole officer was so sure that the Florida Parole Commission would release me from supervision. We drove down and stayed with Brother Don and Nita in Tallahassee and Stacy and I went to the hearing. The commission told me that I was doing a super great job, that they were so proud of what I had accomplished, to keep up the good work, and then voted "No Change." That totally knocked the breath out me.

I was stunned and shocked. I walked out of that

place so disappointed and heart broken. I was devastated. In order for me to get involved in Prison Ministry, I really needed this Parole Supervision Release. I cried all the way back to Clarksville, Tennessee. What else could I do? I had done everything that they ask. How devastating and discouraging it all was to me.

It was a very long ride back to Tennessee, and we were both deeply heartbroken. It was one of those "Why God?" moments and the answer just isn't there. Yet even in heartbreak and disappointment His Love and Peace continues to flow in us. ***2 Cor. 4:8-10 "We are troubled on every side, yet not distressed; we are perplexed, but not in despair; Persecuted, but not forsaken; cast down, but not destroyed; Always bearing about in the body the dying of the Lord Jesus, that the life also of Jesus might be made manifest in our body."***

On the way to Clarksville we stopped and visited with Aunt Kathryn, and we decided that we needed to move closer to her. She was family and she was getting up in age and Stacy and I wanted to be there for her. So as we left her house that day we had decided to start working on that plan.

We started building our house in the exact same area that Stacy had picked out while I was still in prison in Florida. It was a lot of hard work as we decided to be our own General Contractor and do as much of the work as possible ourselves. I actually designed the blueprints and drew them myself using the AutoCAD skills I had learned while in the CAD Vocational program in a Florida Prison. This allowed us to design our home the way we wanted it to be. You see it is more than just a house, but a Home, full of the Love, Mercy and Grace of

Jesus Christ. Anyone can build a house, but to build a Home you have to have Christ Jesus as the master builder.

It was a lot of stressful and hard work to have the excavation contractors clear the land, then have the foundation and basement dug out and concrete footings poured, then have the framers come and frame the house, the roofers put on the roof. It was a massive building project for just the two of us, but it was sort of like our entire life, we had been building a relationship and laying a foundation in our love and marriage from the early days of Prison.

Stacy and I had spent hours upon hours over the 17 years of my incarceration and the 15+ years of our friendship and prison engagement sharing our innermost thoughts, our hurts and our joys, our dreams and our plans for a future. Now here we were building a house on the very land that she had picked out years before while I was still sitting in Prison. ***1 Cor. 3:9-11 "For we are labourers together with God: ye are God's husbandry, ye are God's building. According to the grace of God which is given unto me, as a wise master-builder, I have laid the foundation, and another buildeth thereon. But let every man take heed how he buildeth thereupon. For other foundation can no man lay than that is laid, which is Jesus Christ."***

Make sure the foundation of your Life

is built on Christ Jesus!

We were so blessed when Stacy's uncle from Minnesota said that he would come and help us with building the house. He was retired and he asked one of his Vietnam War Air Force buddies to come with him.

His friend and his wife came from Colorado with him to help us. It was a joy to have her uncle and his friend and wife come and spend time with us and help us work on getting the house dried in. They were friends and family that made a lifelong impact on us as well as lifelong memories.

One of the pressing concerns whenever someone moves or relocates is always where will I get a job. This is even more of a concern and challenge for an ex-con and having to face the stigma of their past over and over again. It was such a difficult time when we decided to leave the good job I had at the college and move to be close to my Aunt. I continued to work at Austin Peay as I looked for another job, I really prayed and sought the Lord about it. I applied to several engineering firms, and job positions in Chattanooga and nothing worked out. Then I saw a posting from an engineering firm in Nashville that had a GIS Manager position for an office they were opening in Chattanooga. It was a long shot but I applied and went to the interview and Praise God I got the job.

The Lord showed me that even in the hard times, He is right there behind the scene working things out. We might not always understand it. We don't always know what tomorrow holds, but we know Who Holds tomorrow. God holds our lives and is in control. I had another quote in one of my chain gang Bibles, which are the four Study Bibles I had while in prison. The quote was that "A problem free life does not bring glory to God...but an overcoming one does." That was so true as I look at my life and the struggles we faced over and over and over again. There was also a note from Stacy in my Bible dated August 1990 that she wrote from a visiting park visit one time, and it said "We should never get so caught up with the things of the world that we forget the simplicity of Loving Jesus."

2 Tim. 2:3-4 "Thou therefore endure hardness, as a good soldier of Jesus Christ. No man that warreth entangleth himself with the affairs of this life; that he may please him who hath chosen him to be a soldier."

That Love for Jesus was real in our prison days, and it is real in our lives today. We were seeing the Lord Bless us in ways that we had never imagined. Dreams do come true. After the house was built, I would sit out on our bedroom balcony and was so awed at the awesome view of the beautiful and majestic Tennessee hills and the Tennessee River, I realized the Goodness and Greatness of God and tears of praise and awe would bubble up in my soul. Because not only did I get to see the Tennessee Mountains again I was living everyday overlooking them.

Living our life and seeing dreams come true put such joy in our hearts. Some of the joys that we have experienced include a summer of fun and fully sharing the love of Christ to a small group of youth from a local church that our daughter Bethany was involved in. We spent the entire spring and summer on the lake swimming, ski tubing, camping, and biking, hiking, ATV riding, horseback riding and enjoying the joy of Jesus. We went tubing down the Sequatchie River, we camped and went mountain biking and swimming at Lula Lake on Lookout Mountain. We went camping and tubing on the Hiwassee River and Whitewater Rafting on the famous Ocoee river in Ocoee, Tennessee, hiking in state parks, ATV riding on trails and even took Bethany on several day trips horseback riding in the Tennessee mountain riding trails.

Every chance I get I want to reach out to young people to help share my story to try my best to keep young people from walking down the same path I have been down. I have dedicated my life to minister and share the redemption and freedom that can only come in finding a relationship with Jesus. We love to speak to young people as well as to the homeless, we like to talk to people in drug rehabs, prisons, jails, juvenile detention centers. I am willing to go anywhere I am invited as long as I can share the truth about the freedom I have found in Christ.

There is Hope and Jesus is the Anchor of my soul.

Our house! More than a house: A HOME!

Whitewater Rafting with the youth group

Debbie and Gary Gibbens with Mickey
Panama City Beach, Florida

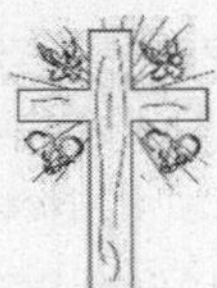

Chapter 30: God on the Mountain is still God in the Valley

I am sure as sure as I can be that God blesses and works in our lives no matter how messed up or busted up our lives may be. I just know that He is able to reach down into the gutters of our sinful lives and pick us up out of the gutters. He is able to reach down into the dark valleys of our broken lives, broken dreams and disappointments and pick us up.

There is a Southern Gospel song that the McKamy's Gospel group sings titled "God on the Mountain" The song shares how that God on the Mountain is STILL GOD IN THE VALLEY.

We would go back to those Florida Parole hearings over and over and over again. I was on parole for 18 years and 9 times or more I would hear them say No, and cry all the way back home to Tennessee. Finally in February of 2016 they finally said yes and released me from Parole. That was a joyous day in my life and I could not contain myself. When the commissioners were voting and I could tell they were going to release me from parole supervision, I was about to jump out of my seat.

Ken Cooper, one of my ex-inmate U.C.I. prison brothers was sitting next to me on one side and Stacy on the other, I was so excited I almost squeezed Ken's leg until I left marks. Stacy was on the other side trying to tell me to be quiet because she was scared to death they would change their mind if they saw how emotional I was. When we left from the hearing, I was outside the Parole Commission Building walking up and down the parking lot Praising God! Crying and shouting Hallelujah thank you JESUS!

My thoughts were now I can go wherever and whenever God leads me, I can go full steam into the Prisons. I called Scott Heburn from the parking lot and rejoiced that the doors were going to open for us to go into the Prisons and see lives changed. We called Debbie and Gary the prison ministry volunteers who had been our faithful friends for years, and of course Stacy's mom who has been a big support to us over all the years. We wanted to let everyone know the good news.

The major joy of my soul was that now I could get back into more prisons and see God use me to share the love of Christ and shine the light of the Gospel into the darkness of prisoners and drug and alcohol recovery programs. How crazy is that to realize that I begged God all those years to get me out prison, now here I am begging Him to get me back into prisons so I can share the Glorious Gospel of JESUS CHRIST.

YES PRAISE GOD! God on the Mountain is STILL GOD IN THE VALLEY!

That has become a precious promise to my heart and mine and Stacy's lives. It is a living testimony of a God who cares and loves us so very much. So much that Jesus went to the cross for us. He took our place for the Bible says “For the wages of sin is death, but the gift of God is eternal life through Jesus Christ our Lord.” Romans 6:23 Jesus suffered and died on Calvary for you and me. That is love glorified, that is love magnified.

There is a worship song that is often sung in Church and I just love it as it speaks deep to my heart and soul. It is Lord Prepare me to be a Sanctuary:

> *“Lord, prepare me to be a sanctuary*
> *Pure and holy, tried and true*
> *With thanksgiving, I'll be a living*
> *Sanctuary for You”*

Chaplain Paulk back at Apalachee Correctional Institution used to preach that "it is not we need more of God, but rather that God needs more of us" That is my heart and soul's desire today, as it was yesterday to be a Living Sanctuary for the Lord. To see God move on the hearts of men and women in jails, prisons and drug and alcohol recovery programs, in the homeless missions and on the streets as the devil has robbed and destroyed their lives as Satan battles for their souls to drag them into an eternal hell.

I have tasted of the sweet honey of God’s Amazing and Glorious Grace and I know what it means to be REDEEMED! To be set free and to live in the joy and peace of the Lord Jesus Christ. I know the Lord Jesus Christ will reach down into the nasty gutters of our lives and pull us up out of the cesspool of sin. He did it for me, and He will do it for you!

You might think you have gone too far, you have done too much, that you are beyond the hope of Grace in Christ. But you are Loved by Christ Jesus, and He is the one and the only one that can truly Help you. No matter where you are, no matter where you have been or what you have done, the price that Jesus paid through his shed Blood can cleanse you from your sin and His overflowing glorious Love is reaching out to you.

God Loves you and wants to REDEEM you, to rescue you from the slave master of Hell and break the chains of Hell upon your life.

Life is not over. Your life is not over and God is not finished with you. I believe that God has a purpose and a plan for your life and that is beyond the drug and alcohol addictions, the chains and shackles of your past. The past failure and sin bondages and sinful habits of your past is over.

Your past does not have to define your future. God takes us as we are and redeems us. He is able! Abundantly able to turn our past into something so much more. I can testify that God changes LIVES, and that is the most powerful truth on earth today. When all else fails, when nothing and no one seems to be able to help you or fix you. God can and will.

Jesus has paid the price in full for our salvation. He offers you a full pardon if you'll receive it, simply, humbly and sincerely. He genuinely loves you and this love is demonstrated through Calvary's cross, manifested through the blood Jesus Christ shed for you. He is willing and ready to help you, deliver and rescue you wherever you are right now.

He will take you from your Rock Bottom to the Rock of Calvary. That is what he did for me and He will do it for you. Trusting Jesus with your broken, busted up life will be the greatest choice you ever made in your life. Trust Him! Obey Him! Please! Listen to him knocking at your heart's door. Open the door of your heart and give Him your soul.

Christ Jesus is the true Stepping Stone to Freedom. *John 8:36 "If the Son therefore shall make you free, ye shall be free indeed!"*

"There is no pit so deep, that He is not deeper."

"GRACE WINS! EVERYTIME!"

Mickey preaching @ Walker State Prison, Georgia Nov. 2016

Mickey & Stacy On the Firing Line for Christ. August 2016

Mickey @A.C.I. after Prison Ministry

Mickey & Stacy in the mountains of Tennessee

Mickey's view from the bedroom balcony.

The ABC's of Salvation and Receiving the Grace of Gods is simply and sincerely:

A- Admit you're a Sinner; Romans. 3:12; 3:23; 6:23

B- Believe Christ died for your sin; John 3:16; Romans. 5:8-9

C- Confess this to God; Romans 10:9-10; 1 John 1:9; Proverbs 28:13

Trusting Jesus to Save you and Change you as you open the closed door your heart and soul to Him. Revelations 3:20 " Behold, I stand at the door, and knock: if any man hear my voice, and open the door, I will come in to him, and will sup with him, and he with me."

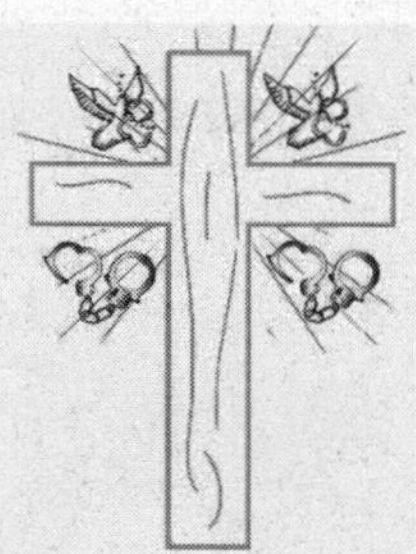

Set Free To Serve Ministries
Evangelist Dr. Mickey Park, Dminn.
P.O. Box 253
New Hope, TN. 37380
http://www.setfreetoserveministry.org
email: **setfree@setfreetoserveministry.org**

Ps. 25:3 No one who hopes in you will ever be put to shame.